Let's just say that we entrepreneurs aren't always the most relaxed people. It's tough to run a business. But Dr. Nadine Greiner breaks it all down for us in this seminal book. I recommend it to my clients and to everybody.

—Doug Bend, legal counsel for entrepreneurs

Dr. Nadine has written a valuable guide for all leaders, covering the broad array of challenges leaders must face, and providing thoughtful guidance on each issue. Whether you are a seasoned leader, or just beginning your journey, you will find excellent advice for leading in our changing world.

—Dr. Paul DeChant, deputy chief health officer,
IBM Watson Health / Simpler Healthcare

This book does an artful job of conveying the tools and processes that keep CEOs like me awake at night. My team and I have engaged Nadine throughout the years to assist us with critical matters. I recommend it highly.

—Bimal Patel, CEO and president, Epic Care

The workforce is changing at a high-rail-train speed, and keeping our employee experience positive and productive is key. Yet, due to societal, health, economic, family, work, and other reasons, our employees and leaders are often stressed. This book helped me understand where my organization and I stand. The tools here are well presented and best in class. Bravo to Nadine for an inspiring and practical book for leaders at all levels.

—Debbie Shotwell, chief people officer, Saba Software

Running an EAP in Silicon Valley, we see that along with the extreme drive for achievement also comes extreme stress. Never before has there been a better time for leaders to receive Nadine's practical, brilliant message. Starting with an honest look at oneself, leaders have the potential to influence an entire industry and squelch the dangerous trend of seeing stress as a badge of honor.

—Cecile Currier, CEO,
CONCERN: An Employee Assistance Program

Having had the privilege of working with Nadine to enhance my career growth, I am excited about this book. Nadine's book takes us deep into defining, handling, and preventing stress in physical, emotional, and mental ways. This book is full of actionable, concrete advice that is easy to implement. I highly recommend this book to any leader who suffers stress.
Bravo, Dr. Nadine!

—Jesus Saucedo, MD, MBA

I have observed that those of us who work in the field of climate change have multiple stressors ranging from how we coalesce to mitigate the effects of climate change to advancing the conversation about the harm we are doing. It is stressful to be killing ourselves and our generations to come. This book will help us by providing individual and organizational solutions. I only wish it had been available to us sooner.

—Warner Chabot, CEO, San Francisco Estuary Institute

Having worked with Nadine, I had to laugh when I read about her "wave to stress." I immediately pictured her waving her hand, with her big charismatic smile. I, myself, have had to contend with stress during my time in the Air Force, having retired as a Chief Master Sargent. I wish I had her book and workshops with me then for my team and for myself.

—Tom Fenyoe, director of talent acquisition, Dignity Health

I design and implement programs to alleviate and prevent stress for our workforce. These programs are costly and difficult to implement. But, as Dr. Nadine Greiner points out, not implementing them is even more costly. Her book has many pieces of great advice and real examples about how organizations can support their workforce.

—Sharawn Connors, vice president of global total rewards and diversity & inclusion, Flex

I had the joy of working with Dr. Greiner through some organizational changes that were stressful for my team as a whole and for individual team members. This book captures some of what I learned from her directly about her insights about the physiological impact of stress and the tips to not only handle but to prevent it. I now apply these lessons in my work to address the impact of toxic stress in vulnerable communities.

—Jim Hickman, CEO, Better Health East Bay

I follow Nadine's work, and I always feel inspired and informed by her insights into leadership and culture. I appreciate learning from a truly skilled practitioner with real-world experience. And there are few skills more valuable for leaders than learning to effectively manage one's own stress to perform at the highest level.

—Mark Fisher, owner,
Mark Fisher Fitness and Business for Unicorns

It seems that stress comes hand-in-hand with being an employer. I enjoyed reading Dr. Greiner's approach to building resilience in the leadership ranks as well as the workforce. The costs of health and welfare benefits are rising each year, in large part due to stress and associated behaviors. Her chapters on self-care made me reflect personally and encouraged me to start a deeper conversation with a couple of my colleagues. This is a powerful book. I recommend it highly.

—Jane Moyer, chief human resources officer, Northeastern University

I had the pleasure of working with Dr. Nadine Greiner, and I am happy to see her putting to the page some of what she has shared with us in person.

—Kirsten Haithcox, senior director of people, Apple

I have learned as a leader that while the effects of stress can single-handedly handicap organizations, stress starts with the individual. And Dr. Nadine's book does a powerful job at addressing stress both at the individual and organizational levels.

—Renaldo Juanso, executive director of public advocacy, Kaiser Permanente

This is a delightful book, full of revealing tests and insightful advice. I had the pleasure of working with Nadine, and I highly recommend her book, too.

—David Goldberg, MD

My team at work is challenged by stress every day. This is the nature of our work. I found Dr. Nadine Greiner's book helpful and an easy read.

—Laura Heinz, CEO, Stanford Youth Solutions

With any change comes resistance and stress. Working as an organization and individually with Dr. Greiner, we have learned how to channel resistance and stress and how to strengthen our organizational resiliency. This book offers practical guidance about individual stress but also powerful lessons in overall leadership.

—James McCaughey, CEO, Bay Medical Management, LLC

As leaders are called to solve more complex issues faster and with a leaner staff, I keep a look out for leader stress and burnout in my colleagues. Dr. Nadine Greiner's chapters on talent review, succession planning, and the organizational costs of stress were singing my tune. This is a pivotal book at a pivotal moment in time.

—Cindy Johnson, chief human resources officer,
Providence Healthcare Network

Nobody can deny that stress has become an epidemic. That's why I recommend Dr. Nadine Greiner's book. She is a delight to work with, and her voice rings clearly through the pages.

—Micheal Pope, CEO, ASEB (Alzheimer's Services of the East Bay)

Leading a workforce is part art, part science, and 100 percent self-leadership. This book gives ample advice and real-life examples on how to do this in a reliable way. This is a powerful book for leaders at all levels.

—Maynard Jenkins, vice president of human resources, Sutter Health

As Nadine points out in this fascinating book, stress is multigenerational as well as situationally contagious. Having worked with Nadine, I was pleased to see that she has committed her work to paper and that her readers can benefit from her research and experience.

—David Newell, president and CEO, PromiseShip, Annie E. Casey
Foundation (AECF) Children and Family Fellowship

Nadine has written a solid book packed with practical advice, tips, and tricks to overcome stress. Having enjoyed Dr. Nadine's short articles online, I am impressed finding the same clarity and accessibility in a full-length book on a challenging subject.

—Kirby Sack, CEO and owner, Sack Properties,
Kirby Sack Properties Inc.

This book offers accessible advice for those who are confronted with stress in their personal lives and at work. Running a small business in San Francisco, I found Nadine's tips on engaging employees and bringing out the best in the culture resonated with what my team and I are always striving for. Thank you for a great book, Nadine.

—Kathleen Kennedy, owner, Quality Eyecare

Nadine is an expert at identifying, quantifying, and fixing human problems and internal challenges. In my roles as an entrepreneur and a leader, I found the sections on leadership development, performance, and culture particularly helpful.

—Patrick Browning, vice president & medical director of specialty services, Magellan Health

I oversee a lot of money and millions of customer transactions. Even with automation, it's the people who run the show. When the people are stressed, things do not go well. This is where Dr. Nadine Greiner's book comes in. She has created a book packed full of solutions for personal well-being to company performance. Thank you, Nadine!

—Karen Introcaso, CEO,
Kaiperm Diablo Federal Credit Union

I live in the moment, yet my job entails planning and building contingencies for the future in a rapidly changing field where the stakes are high. But Nadine has helped me when I work with her and now in this book. The sections on making time to think and reflection are concepts I work on with my team and personally. Thank you, Nadine!

—Will Hahn, director of strategy & business development,
Sutter Health

Want the secret to managing your stress? Read this book! It is filled with great tools to use in work and life. Your leadership will improve and your life will be longer when your stress is managed. Thank you for the best book in stressful times, Nadine!

—Surani Hayre-Kwan, director of professional practice and nursing excellence, Office of Patient Experience at Samuel Merritt University

My patients, just like all of us, carry multiple stressors. This book has given me some practical ideas about how to help them. I am also a physician leader in charge of large capital projects, and I found the chapters on how to navigate organizational stress very helpful.

—Stuart Menaker, family physician

The chapters on the physiological impacts of stress are very well laid out and cathartic. This is a clear call to action, not only for the reader, but to society. In her book, Dr. Nadine Greiner tackles the important questions around what we can do to help others and to help ourselves.

—Candy Canga-Picar, chief nursing officer, St. Charles Health System

Dr. Greiner's exercises and suggestions for changing one's response to stress apply equally to people in nonprofit settings, in workgroups or on teams of any kind, even to solitary activists working to effect social justice and legislative change—anyone who needs to collaborate or cooperate with others to get things done. This book is just the ticket for self-assessment and reflection that we all can use to increase our productivity and reduce our stress in our stressful world.

—Dr. Jamison Green, author, educator, corporate consultant, and legislative provocateur

stress-less
leadership

how to lead
in business and in life

dr. nadine greiner

Entrepreneur Press®

Entrepreneur Press, Publisher
Cover Design: Andrew Welyczko
Production and Composition: Eliot House Productions
Illustrations by Shana Cinquegrana

This publication is designed to provide accurate and authoritative information
in regard to the subject matter covered. It is sold with the understanding that
the publisher is not engaged in rendering legal, accounting, or other professional
services. If legal advice or other expert assistance is required, the services of a
competent professional person should be sought.

Entrepreneur Press® is a registered trademark of Entrepreneur Media, Inc.

Library of Congress Cataloging-in-Publication Data
  Names: Greiner, Nadine, author.
  Title: Stress-less leadership\ : how to lead your organization and your life /
    by Nadine Greiner.
  Description: Irvine, California: Entrepreneur Media, Inc., [2019]
  Identifiers: LCCN 2019013450| ISBN 978-1-59918-650-4 (alk. paper) |
    ISBN 1-59918-650-0 (alk. paper)
  Subjects: LCSH: Leadership. | Job stress. | Stress management.
  Classification: LCC HD57.7 .G7438 2019 | DDC 658.4/092—dc23
  LC record available at https://lccn.loc.gov/2019013450

Printed in the United States of America

23 22 21 20 19   10 9 8 7 6 5 4 3 2 1

You're born. Then you die.
This book is for you, for the part in between.

contents

acknowledgments

Ok, yes, I have to admit it, this book was stressful. So thank you to everybody who put up with me and didn't say, "What, another book?" Queen of Everything, I owe it all to you. And finally, thank you to the love of my life, mon Petit Prince.

Author proceeds of this book go to the protection and love of animals.

foreword by
marshall goldsmith

*#1 leadership thinker, executive coach,
and new york times bestselling author*

S tress eats us up. Stress kills us. Stress is a poison in our
society, and I see the devastating impact of stress firsthand
in my practice as a coach and consultant to the highest
performing organizations. In fact, if I am not rigorous with
my own self-care and daily habits, even my own stress will
build up.

In this book, Dr. Greiner has gifted us with a practical and actionable solution to combat stress. Using a wave of the hand to approach stress, with an emphasis on each finger, we learn how to be better stewards of ourselves and our organizations. The science behind stress is particularly helpful as Dr. Greiner's clinical psychology background helps us understand our relationship to our bodies, and this serves as a platform to freeing ourselves from the negative mental and emotional impacts of stress.

In my own work with leaders within the worlds of industry, education, politics, nonprofits, and other fields, I have witnessed stress ranging from mild to severe. In this book, I found many useful tools and techniques. One that sticks with me now is her simple but effective construct to name the four different kinds of stress: time, anticipatory, situational, and encounter stress.

Time stress happens when we are anxious about not having enough time. Leaders can feel under the gun when they have more tasks than time, looming deadlines, and piles of unread emails and a calendar full of meetings.

Anticipatory stress involves our thoughts and feeling about the future. We might think or comment about a future event, and say, "All that can go wrong will." When we do this, we have a negative set of assumptions (conscious or unconscious) and a negative set of corresponding thoughts. And this leads us to experience anticipatory stress, which results in a set of negative emotions involving stress, worry, and perhaps some physical symptoms as well as a rapid heartbeat.

Situational stress is when leaders are surrounded by a seemingly no-win situation, such as lay-offs, a market drop, or a mistake. They experience "danger" on a physical and emotional level, and they feel they lack control. The key here is that they might be catastrophizing or exaggerating the implications of their situation and feeling ten times more fear or pressure than the situation actually calls for. But it seems real. And part of it is.

Finally, *encounter stress* is experienced by leaders when their contact with colleagues, stakeholders, vendors, or other entities causes stress, discomfort, or anxiety. Leaders may experience this type of stress during encounters with an over-demanding boss, a colleague who is overtly critical, or a board member who demeans them.

We are all different. Yet, the human reaction to stress is common to all of us around the globe. The stress reaction is a sequence of bodily effects that triggers the fight-or-flight response. Adrenaline, cortisol, and norepinephrine (the so-called "stress hormones") are released. Many researchers refer to this as the "Stone Age" reaction because, as you might recall from history classes, the fight-or-flight reaction enabled our nomadic ancestors to handle life-threatening situations, such as an enemy tribe or bear attack. Unfortunately, now, leaders don't just experience the fight-or-flight response when their lives are threatened. An unexpected late-night email from a boss or customer can easily activate it. Therefore, leaders and their teams experience it constantly. Stress is contagious.

As my life has unfolded, I have clarified and narrowed my own mission. My mission is simple. I want to help successful people achieve positive, lasting change and behavior—for themselves, their people, and their teams. This book does just that, which is why I am delighted for you, as the reader, to now have access to Dr. Greiner's seminal work on stress.

challenge accepted

As an executive consultant and coach, I wake up each day with one goal: to help my clients tackle the challenges they are facing. For some of my clients, that may mean building a new team or enterprise. For some, it's clinching their next promotion. For others, it's powering through a new line of business or a hiring freeze. All my clients face different challenges, and some of their turmoil is caused by positive changes.

Yet there's one common thread that binds them: Almost all are experiencing stress. That stress has become part of their DNA. They've accepted it as a necessary evil, a way of life—even a badge of honor.

But stress has become a toxic force in most professionals' work and personal lives. Most difficult business challenges require leaders to have a reliable way to handle stress, by tackling the necessary stressors for themselves and their teams and preventing the unnecessary ones. Day after day, I was seeing many of my clients feeling unable to cope. I am an executive coach with a clinical psychologist background, so my clients felt our time together was healing and helpful, but since I am not with them 24 hours a day, I needed more tools to help them. I needed homework and resources to help my clients deal with high stress levels between meetings.

I scoured the web. The internet has all the answers, right? Not in this case. Even after digging through countless pages of research, I found nothing. At many points in my quest, I became hopeful that I'd found my needle in a haystack. But time and time again, I was too optimistic. Sure, there are books and other resources on stress and trauma. And there is certainly no shortage of books on leadership. Yet in the end, I emerged empty-handed. I couldn't find anything that addressed both stress *and* leadership. And so I set out to write this book.

If you're reading or listening to this book, you're probably a manager, a leader, or an entrepreneur. You have responsibilities. You're working long hours in a complex environment. Deadlines keep getting shorter and shorter. And you're more emotionally and digitally connected to your work than ever before. Work-life balance has become a distant fantasy.

I have a very specific goal in writing this book. I want to help you eradicate the *unnecessary* stress from your life and help you address the inevitable stress you must face. Stress is a fact of life. In small doses, it can even be a gift, a powerful stimulant of peak performance. There's a reason this book is called *Stress-Less Leadership* and not *Stress-Free Leadership*. This book won't help you eliminate all stress from your life. But it will help you reduce the stressors you're facing and minimize your negative responses to stress.

The results will be far-reaching. Your life will improve, and so will the lives of the hundreds of people you manage, work with, and interact with each day. And there will be a domino effect. All your second, third, fourth, and higher connections will benefit, too. The cumulative effects will positively impact your community, country, and the world.

My ask is to consider this book a challenge to learn new ways to handle stressors and stress. If you accept it fully, you can incite a stress-less revolution.

who am i?

Who am I to tackle such an important subject? I like to think of my expertise as a unique "trifecta" of skills. It's this trifecta that qualifies me.

First, I'm a psychologist with a doctorate in clinical psychology, specializing in trauma. I am recognized as an expert in understanding and treating stress, and I work with my local district attorney's office on some of their most difficult clinical cases.

Second, I've held multiple senior leadership positions in private and publicly traded companies, and I have a doctorate in organization development. When I was 38, I was hired as the CEO of a health-care company and held other executive positions. During my decades of executive coaching and consulting, I've helped more than a thousand clients become more effective and fulfilled in their jobs.

Third, my human resources background helps me navigate the HR and legal issues that affect all companies. Stress is not experienced in a vacuum. My mediation and arbitration skills allow me to facilitate productive conversations among different stakeholders that lead to change. Taken together, my fluency in stress, leadership, and tactical execution uniquely positions me to write this book.

what to expect

Business books can be a bore. They can be long and full of unnecessary words. As with my previous book, *The Art of Executive Coaching*, I didn't want to go down that path. I wanted to write a business book that was an enjoyable read filled with tools, techniques, tips, and solutions that addressed the personal, team, organizational, cultural, and global effects of stress. I realized long ago that people learn best when they are relaxed, engaged, and having fun. So the book you're holding is a short one that is jam-packed with action-driven solutions. Hopefully you'll have fun reading it.

The book starts by defining stress and giving you a detailed overview of the types of stressors and stress most companies, leaders, and employees encounter. There are checklists and a test that will give you an idea of where you stand in terms of your own stress. You will gain insight into what kind of personality type you are and how you handle stress today. Once you know how too much stress can negatively impact your health, your career, and your life, as well as those around you, you can hone in on relevant aspects in the remaining chapters, which delve into preventative measures at the individual and organizational levels.

The framework I use to walk you through these preventative steps has five aspects, or "fingers." Pointing or wagging your finger at stress will not get rid of it, but you can use the "Five Finger Wave" to say goodbye to stress. In this book, you'll read about five specific techniques you can use to de-stress your life and leadership. Each finger is an area impacted by stress: cognitive, emotional, interpersonal, physical, and spiritual. For each of the main fingers, there are four or five stress solutions you can apply to your own work and life. I have also included real-life examples from well-known leaders in the world, and from my work with my own clients.

Stress must first be addressed at the individual level. Because nearly half of workers say they need help in learning how to manage stress, and 42 percent say their co-workers need such help.[1] That's why in the first part of this book, you'll have an opportunity to diagnose your own stress levels and tendencies. You'll learn about how stress affects various leadership behaviors, and develop an action plan to tackle your stress.

The later chapters of this book focus on helping you adopt the best interventions for handling stress throughout the enterprise. Because stress affects employees across teams and dampens employee and overall company performance, this book proposes leadership best practices to prevent stress in a more structural and proactive way. There are many ways to run a business, and this book helps focus on the highest impact interventions to reduce and prevent stress. You will also learn about how specific leadership practices enable the company to have an effective approach to transform stress and use it to your advantage.

As you work your way through the book, you'll discover research and solutions from many different fields. I have included the best of the current research and added my own expertise and experience. It's all in one place, saving you a lot of time and trouble in your quest to conquer individual and organizational stress. Throughout the book, you'll also find quizzes and reflection questions. These are meant to engage you, to provoke your thinking, to help you ascertain where you are with certain topics, and to motivate you to take action. Feel free to write all over the book. Some of my favorite books are all marked up, including some that others gave me with their own writing already in them.

I can't promise that you'll always be able to hit your optimal level of stress (again, a little stress is a good thing). But I can promise that you will be vastly more successful and joyful when you embrace and apply the methods, tips, and tricks in this book. And I do promise that, as you read this book, you'll realize you are not alone. Indeed, there is ample hope, there are a plethora of solutions, and you can make immediate, sustained progress.

chapter 1

let's set the record straight

Y ou're no stranger to stress. It is a key part of your daily routine. You pride yourself on your ability to cope with it; you wouldn't have gotten where you are today without that ability. But are you really coping? Are you really conquering stress?

Because stress has become such a big part of your life, it's easy to dismiss it as normal. While it's ubiquitous, stress isn't inevitable. In this chapter, you'll gain a better understanding of stress. You'll learn about the common symptoms and causes of stress. You'll learn how stress affects the workplace. You'll learn not only how to combat stress but also how to prevent it from derailing your personal and professional life in the first place. Finally, you'll learn about the benefits of stress (yes, there are some), and most importantly, you'll learn how to use it to your advantage.

what is stress?

Let's start with the basics. Stress can be defined as any stimulus that produces a marked and negative stress response in the body. Imagine you awaken from sleep in the middle of the night to the smell of smoke. Your heart pounding and adrenaline pumping, you investigate the source of the smell. If you find a fire that's small enough to be contained, you're ready to fight it. If it is too large to tackle, you're ready to wake your family and flee the house. The stress you experience in these situations depends wholly on external factors.

Stress comes in different flavors. In his 1979 book *Stress and the Manager* (Touchstone), stress-reduction expert Karl Albrecht defined four common flavors of stress: time stress, anticipatory stress, situational stress, and encounter stress. Let's unpack each one.

Time stress occurs when people worry about time, or (more likely) the lack thereof. Time-strapped supervisors, managers, and executives are no stranger to this type of stress. They worry about the piles of tasks and activities on their plates. They fear they won't live up to their potential. Impending deadlines only fuel the time-stress fire.

Anticipatory stress relates to one's thoughts of the future. Leaders experience anticipatory stress when they voice a concern about a future event (e.g., an upcoming presentation or board meeting), or about the future in general. Remember Murphy's Law? "If anything can go wrong, it will."

Situational stress occurs when individuals find themselves in a scary or dangerous situation where they feel they lack control. A house fire is a prime example. In the case of leaders, situational stress often occurs when executives lose face. Their status drops (as the result of a layoff or termination) or they fall out of favor (as the result of a failed presentation or pitch), for example.

Finally, *encounter stress* occurs when interactions with co-workers, business partners, or other professionals cause feelings of uneasiness. Interacting with a toxic and demeaning boss or with a highly judgmental co-worker can create a ripe breeding ground for encounter stress.

Human reactions to stress are quite remarkable. The stress response is a pattern of bodily reactions that triggers a fight-or-flight response. As Marshall noted earlier, many researchers call the response a "Stone Age" reaction and for good reason. As you probably learned in history class, the fight-or-flight response originated as a survival mechanism that allowed our hunter-gatherer ancestors to respond quickly to life-threatening situations, like a tiger or a pack of wolves. Today, people don't just experience the fight-or-flight response when their lives are in danger. They experience it constantly. An unexpected late-night email from a boss or customer can easily activate it.

The stress response is created in your brain. When you perceive a threat such as a potential house fire, your amygdala—a group of neurons in your brain—sends an SOS-type distress signal to the hypothalamus, your brain's command center. This causes you to immediately sense the potential for danger. The hypothalamus then activates the sympathetic nervous system by transmitting signals to the adrenal glands. Adrenaline, cortisol, and norepinephrine (the so-called "stress hormones") are released. As they flush and circulate throughout your body, they trigger a tsunami of sorts. Your heartbeat escalates, and your blood pressure rises. To fight the perceived threat, a flood of oxygen is transmitted to your brain and your five senses become more discriminating. Sugars and fats are released into your bloodstream for added energy, and the strength of your muscles is enhanced.

While these responses are physical, their cause is subjective. Stress can be real or imagined. It is not based on objective reality. Instead, it's based on your perceptions and how stress is processed by the brain. A stressor for you may not be a stressor for your co-worker. This means that to some extent, you can choose your stress response by choosing your beliefs about the stressor.

I will always remember the time a client called to tell me he was laid off from his job. I immediately said I was sorry to hear that. He replied that he was in fact delighted because he was thinking about leaving anyway and just needed a push. So to some extent, events are neutral. It is your own beliefs about the event that bring on a positive response or a negative stress response. In other words, it's your belief system that codes you to respond as an optimist or a pessimist.

are you an optimist or a pessimist?

Optimists focus on finding the positive in life. They are future-oriented and see each day as a new opportunity. They tend to thrive in adversity and look at obstacles as challenges. This doesn't mean that optimists never have a bad day. It just means their first impulse is to find the positives that surround them.

Pessimists, on the other hand, are prone to see the negatives in life. They often don't feel like they are in control of their fate. They tend to focus on past events and often see themselves at the mercy of their environment. Unlike optimists, who are usually looking for possibilities, pessimists often look for problems. They tend to take situations personally. Take the quiz in Figure 1.1 on page 5 to see how you fare.

when does stress become harmful?

People often associate stress with its harmful effects. This type of stress is called *distress*, and it triggers negative cognitive, behavioral, and physical consequences. Stress can also have a stimulating effect. This type of stress is called *eustress*. Eustress can be triggered when a person encounters a new experience, like working with a new team or starting a new job. The desire to succeed at something often triggers stress. While the stress you experience when encountering

You probably already have a good idea about whether you are an optimist or a pessimist. Reply with true ("T") or false ("F") to the following statements to gauge where you stand on the optimism/pessimism scale.

Statement	True ("T") or False ("F")
Life is a struggle.	
I'm not looking forward to tomorrow.	
Good things don't usually last.	
When I wake up, I usually don't plan on having a good day.	
You're late for work because of traffic. You assume the entire day is ruined.	

If you responded with three or more "T"s, you skew towards the pessimistic side.

FIGURE 1.1 **quiz: are you an optimist or a pessimist?**

new opportunities and challenges can make you anxious, the positive aspects of the situation often outweigh the ill effects.

Think about a time when you felt on top of the world. Perhaps you were given a standing ovation after delivering a keynote speech. Perhaps someone complimented you on making a presentation or for your contributions in a meeting. Perhaps you won first prize in a triathlon or completed your first 5K run. How did you feel before the event? You probably felt invigorating butterflies in your gut. This is eustress.

What determines whether stress results in distress or eustress? At what point does a challenge, opportunity, or event morph into a stressful situation? It turns out there is an important inflection point. According to the Yerkes-Dodson law, an individual's performance increases with some level of stress but only up to a point. After stress reaches a point of optimal arousal, performance decreases, as you can see in Figure 1.2 on page 6.

The exact shape of the curve may be slightly different than the one shown here. As you can see in Figure 1.2, your position on the curve varies based on the complexity and familiarity of the task.

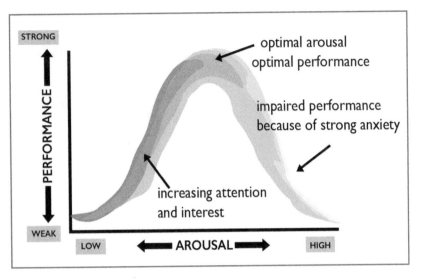

FIGURE 1.2 **yerkes-dodson law**[i]

Difficult or unfamiliar tasks demand higher levels of arousal and result in taller peaks.

How do you know when you've hit the inflection point? This requires some work on your part. Pin down the exact moment when you first felt unable to meet a challenge—that's when you reached the top of the stress mountain.

For example, imagine that your boss has just assigned you to a new project. Shortly afterward, you realize you don't have the resources to execute it properly. Perhaps you haven't been given enough funding or enough manpower. What's certain is that you're destined for failure, and despite your valiant attempts to secure additional resources, you're given the cold shoulder. This type of environment is the perfect breeding ground for stress. You feel hopeless and the problem seems beyond your control. These two characteristics are common to almost all stressful situations: fear of an unsuccessful outcome and a sense that the situation is beyond your control.

chronic vs. acute stress

In many cases, stress is short-lived and lasts only as long as the stress-inducing project or event. Once you've completed the project or the event has concluded, your stress levels return to normal. You breathe a sigh of relief as your body recuperates. This is an example of acute or short-term stress. Delivering a presentation at work, for example, is a source of acute stress.

Your body is built to handle short bursts of high stress during emergencies. It's not meant to cope with stress over long periods of time. When stressful conditions endure, your body begins to break down. When stress hormones are released consistently over the span of days, weeks, or even months, they begin to upset the delicate balance of bodily processes. If your company is getting squashed by the competition or experiencing a nosedive in revenue, this may create a constant source of ongoing stress. This type of stress is no longer acute. It is considered chronic or long-term stress. Take the quiz in Figure 1.3 below to see what kind of stress you have.

Using the table below, classify the situations described in the first four rows as causing either chronic ("C") or acute ("A") stress. Then, in the last two rows, describe a chronic and an acute stressor you've experienced in the past or are experiencing currently.

Situation	Chronic ("C") or Acute ("A") Stress
1. Delivering a presentation to a large group of strangers	
2. The death of a loved one	
3. Getting stuck in traffic and missing an early morning meeting	
4. Ongoing marital problems	
	"C"
	"A"

Solutions: 1. "A," 2. "C," 3. "A," 4. "C"

FIGURE 1.3 **quiz: is your stress chronic or acute?**

The effects of acute and chronic stress can be vast. Stress has been shown to play a role in everything from the common cold to cancer. As sophisticated as our cognitive processes are, humans are still mammals with mammalian bodies. Cortisol is a key contributor to many stress effects, suppressing the functions that your body considers unnecessary in an emergency, while it shifts all its resources toward dealing with the life-threatening event. Stress impacts many bodily systems, including the respiratory system, the cardiovascular system, the nervous system, and even the reproductive system.

Like the types of stress, the effects of stress come in many different flavors. They can be grouped into four primary buckets: cognitive, emotional, physical, and behavioral effects.

cognitive effects of stress

I chose to label this section "cognitive" rather than "thinking" because, although it can sound quite clinical, cognition encompasses much more than thought. It encompasses all the mental processes you are not aware of. It's kind of like your heart beating whether or not you are thinking about it.

Stress can take a heavy toll on your cognitive functions. In extreme circumstances, there is a clear link between chronic stress and a greater incidence of psychiatric disorders. Stress has also been linked to Alzheimer's disease and other forms of dementia. It has even been shown to reduce the size of the brain. Ouch!

mental slowdown

Mental slowdown is a common cognitive effect of stress. It slows down your brain's processing speed, meaning it takes you longer to process new information, make decisions, and interact with colleagues. You may become frustrated by your lower levels of productivity, which may result in a loss of enjoyment at work. Even the brightest leaders and employees can fall victim to mental slowdown. Sometimes people experiencing mental slowdown are viewed as unengaged because their output is delayed and their interactions with others are incomplete. In reality, their brain rewiring just needs some TLC.

difficulty concentrating

Concentration is challenging even when you're at your best. When you're tethered to your devices, distraction can come in many different forms. Stress only adds to the fire. When you struggle to concentrate, you can't focus on tasks that need to be completed, you are easily distracted, your self-esteem erodes, and you waste precious time. Solving problems becomes impossible, conversations become disjointed, and teamwork evades us.

feeling overwhelmed

People feel overwhelmed when they are in a stressful situation—either at home or in the workplace—that just becomes too much for them to deal with. Your brain may start to feel foggy. You may feel paralyzed, have difficulty thinking clearly, or react rashly to situations. It becomes hard to see a way out or a way through your problems.

memory loss or impairment

Stress takes an especially heavy toll on your memory. Individuals facing stress often find themselves becoming forgetful. For leaders especially, this should be concerning. After all, the health of their company depends on their judgment and vision. If workers are impaired in their ability to recall organizational knowledge or even something as trivial as dates and deadlines, their performance levels are likely to plummet.

Use Table 1.1 on page 10 to help you assess whether you may be experiencing the more common symptoms of cognitive stress. As you go about your day, jot down your experiences related to each symptom as they occur as well as your answers to the accompanying questions.

emotional aspects of stress

Stress can also affect your emotions. You'll often experience changes to your personality, causing you to become more irritable or more

Symptom	My Experiences	Reflection Questions	My Response
Mental slowdown		When was the last time you experienced mental slowdown? Did it cause your performance to deteriorate?	
Difficulty concentrating		How often do you find it difficult to concentrate? Are there certain triggers?	
Feeling overwhelmed		When was the last time you felt overwhelmed? How long did the feeling last?	
Memory loss or impairment		When was the last time you noticed your memory had declined? Was it in response to stress? If so, what was the stressor?	

TABLE 1.1 **cognitive stress symptom log**

likely to feel depressed. It can feel like you're riding a roller coaster. And right at the top of the list is irritability.

irritability

Irritability is closely associated with stress. When you feel irritable, you feel agitated and become upset easily. In the workplace, irritability can be especially dangerous. It often causes you to react impulsively or lash out at others. Showing irritation can have negative consequences on your career as this behavior can be perceived as bullying or harassment.

anxiety

Anxiety is a feeling of worry most commonly associated with uncertain events. Often, people fear they will experience the worst. Events at work might elicit a positive response or a negative stress response of anxiety. Examples could include changes in office location, speaking at meetings, layoffs, performance reviews, getting a new assignment or manager, or even getting a promotion. Anxiety can impede cognitive functions and making it difficult to do tasks effectively. Palpitations, tremors, and a feeling of tightening in the chest can be physical manifestations of this feeling.

lack of motivation

Lack of motivation is a common symptom of a negative stress reaction. Even the simplest tasks can feel challenging. In the workplace, a lack of motivation is often revealed in low employee engagement survey results, being tardy on deliverables, and poor-quality work. A good leader can pick up on low motivation quickly and get to the root of the problem. The best leaders know instinctively how to engage and motivate individuals and teams and how to remove barriers to motivation. Once tasks are achieved, motivation builds on itself, and people move from achievement to larger achievement.

helplessness

You might feel helpless when you feel you aren't in control. If this feeling continues over a long period of time, it often causes inaction. In the workplace, helplessness may result in impaired teamwork. It may also result in low levels of creativity and innovation. You can feel so helpless that you stop trying. This erodes your self-confidence, optimism, and sense of belonging.

depression

Depression affects many of us at some point and to some extent. It's a serious mood disorder that results in a severe, prolonged feeling of sadness and a loss of self-esteem and hope. It also tends to cause a loss of interest in daily activities, including work. Ultimately, depression can lead to self-harm or suicide, which is on the rise. High levels of depression in the workplace tend to result in increased use of employee assistance programs (EAPs), increased time off, and increased use of company health plans and other resources.

Use Table 1.2 on page 13 to reflect on your experiences and help you assess how you may have been or may be experiencing the more common symptoms of emotional stress. As you go about your day, jot down your experiences related to each symptom as they occur.

The more you resonate with the symptoms, the higher your stress level likely is. If you identify strongly with three or more symptoms, you're likely experiencing a high level of stress.

Research has found that chromosomes in individuals who are exposed to chronic stress exhibit shorter structures called *telomeres* (the outermost part of the chromosomes). While telomeres shorten with age, the process is accelerated among those who experience stress. It's like you're pressing fast-forward on your life. Shorter telomeres cause cells to age faster, die younger, and take a heavy toll on your emotional well-being.

Stress fundamentally alters brain circuitry and has long-term effects on your mental well-being. If you're exposed to constant stress, you can experience depression, bipolar disorder, and other mental illnesses. The emotional effects of stress are ever-present in the workplace. A 2011 "Attitudes in the American Workplace" survey revealed that 14 percent of workers have an urge to hit their co-workers due to stress.[2] Talk about a morale killer.

physical aspects of stress

Stress also causes a very palpable physical reaction. It can feel like you've been run over by a truck. Your energy levels may take a nosedive. The physical effects of stress can be felt head to toe.

Symptom	My Experiences	Reflection Questions	My Response
Irritability		What are some of the triggers that cause you to feel irritable at home? At work? Are they people? Are they events?	
Anxiety		How often do you feel anxiety? Do you have any strategies currently in place to address it?	
Lack of motivation		When was the last time you felt your motivation levels plummet? Do you feel engaged at work?	
Helplessness		When was the last time you felt helpless? Did it affect your work?	
Depression		When was the last time you felt blue? What was the cause? How long did the feeling last?	

TABLE 1.2 **emotional stress symptom log**

muscle tension

Muscle tension is a type of reflex reaction to stress. It's the body's way of shielding itself from danger. You can feel the effects of stress in the form of nagging or gripping pain in the back of your neck or lower back as you type at your computer. You may tense up in the jaw or brow, sometimes for hours on end. Often you don't notice the muscle tension you're experiencing.

headaches

Headaches and stress are evil twins. The relationship is so strong that it has its own term: "stress headaches" (also called "tension headaches"). Pain is typically felt in both sides of the head and often causes a feeling of tightness in the forehead or the back of the neck.

migraines

According to the American Migraine Foundation, stress is a trigger for migraines in almost 70 percent of people.[3] When the fight-or-flight response is triggered, there's a release of chemicals that causes your blood vessels to change and even dilate, which can set off a migraine.

digestive problems

Stress alters the concentration of stomach acid. This can lead to bloating, cramps, diarrhea, constipation, irritable bowel syndrome, and even peptic ulcers. Peptic ulcers are open sores that develop on

---

a note on migraines

Can you distinguish between a migraine and a regular headache? Many people can't. Here are three ways to differentiate the two.

1. Migraines are mostly felt on one side of the head, while headaches are felt throughout the forehead and/or scalp.

2. Migraines tend to cause intense pulsing or throbbing sensations, whereas headaches cause milder, duller pressure sensations.

3. Migraines are more likely to occur along with other bodily effects, including nausea and dizziness. And are preceded by a visual aura—developing wavy visual sensations and blind spots.

---

the inner lining of the stomach and upper part of the small intestine. Common symptoms include burning stomach pain, feelings of fullness or bloating, heartburn, and intolerance to fatty foods. If you're experiencing a peptic ulcer, stay clear of the doughnuts in the break room. Coffee, alcohol, and tobacco products can worsen symptoms.

diabetes

Psychological stress upsets insulin production in the body, which can lead to diabetes. Diabetes can be difficult to detect. Often individuals don't realize they have diabetes until after long-term damage has been done. Common symptoms include hunger, thirst, frequent urination, itchy skin, and blurred vision.

strokes

A continuous increase in heart rate and consistently high blood pressure levels increase the risk of heart attacks and stroke. Studies have shown that people who face many stressors, ranging from those who survive natural disasters to those who work long hours, are more likely to develop *atherosclerosis*, a buildup of plaque in the arteries. When the plaques break loose from the artery walls, this can cause more extreme blockages in other areas. The result may be a stroke or heart attack. Warning signs for strokes include face drooping, arm weakness, and impaired speech.

heart attacks

Common symptoms of heart attacks include lightheadedness, jaw pain, chest or upper-body discomfort, and shortness of breath. Symptoms, however, are highly gender-specific. Women, in particular, are more likely to experience shortness of breath, nausea and/or vomiting, and back or jaw pain. If you suspect you or someone else is experiencing a heart attack, call 911 immediately. Take the quiz in Figure 1.4 on page 16 to see if you can tell the difference between a heart attack and a stroke.

It can often be difficult to differentiate between heart attacks and strokes, both of which are closely associated with stress. Many of the same physiological phenomena are at play in both cases. Classify the following symptoms according to whether they are more likely to be associated with a heart attack ("H") or a stroke ("S").

Symptom	Heart Attack ("H") or Stroke ("S")
1. Lightheadedness	
2. Jaw pain	
3. Difficulty speaking	
4. Numbness on the left side of the body	

Solutions: 1. "H," 2. "H," 3. "S," 4. "S"

FIGURE 1.4 **quiz: heart attack or stroke?**

heart disease

Stress is a significant risk factor for heart disease. Common symptoms include shortness of breath, increased heartbeat, nausea, dizziness, and sweating. The risk of heart disease is strongly associated with family history. Race and ethnicity are also key factors. Black people, for example, are more susceptible to heart disease than white people. In the U.S., approximately half of all black adults live with some form of cardiovascular disease.[4] Are you genetically at a higher risk for heart disease? People smoke more under stress, which also increases risk.

lowered immune response

Stress raises the number of suppressor T cells, inhibiting the immune system. As a result, the immune system is less able to fight off attackers such as viruses and bacteria. Signs of a weakened immune system include frequent infections, frequent colds and flus, shingles, yeast infections, rheumatoid arthritis, and even warts. Being in close quarters with co-workers, fellow transit commuters, and family only increases the risk.

Use the symptom log in Table 1.3 on page 17 to reflect on your experiences and assess how you may have experienced or may

Symptom	My Experiences	Reflection Questions	My Response
Muscle tension		When was the last time you experienced muscle tension? Where did you feel it? What were you doing?	
Headaches		When was the last time you had a headache? What were you doing?	
Migraines		When was the last time you experienced a migraine? Did you feel it in both sides of your head? How did you know it wasn't a headache?	
Digestive problems		When was the last time you experienced digestive problems? Can you remember a time you experienced digestive problems in response to stress? Did you feel a burning sensation or cramps in your stomach? Did you experience bloating?	
Diabetes		Have you been diagnosed with diabetes? If so, do you have Type 1 or Type 2 diabetes? Do you have a family history of diabetes?	

TABLE 1.3 **physical stress symptom log**

Symptom	My Experiences	Reflection Questions	My Response
Strokes		Do you have a family history of strokes? Have you ever experienced a stroke?	
Heart attacks		Do you have a family history of heart attacks? Have you ever experienced a heart attack?	
Heart disease		Are you genetically at a higher risk for heart disease?	
Lowered immune response		Do you always seem to have a cold? Do you often get a cold after you travel on a plane? Do your wounds take a long time to heal? These may be signs of a weakened immune system.	

TABLE 1.3 **physical stress symptom log,** continued

currently be experiencing the more common symptoms of physical stress. As you go about your day, jot down your experiences related to each symptom as they occur.

behavioral aspects of stress

Stress has a significant influence on your behavior. When you are highly stressed, your cognitive resources are so depleted that you are no longer able to make logical and sound decisions. You often don't feel or act like yourself. Changes to behavior as a result of stress almost always have negative effects.

social withdrawal

Social withdrawal is strongly connected to anxiety and depression. When you feel anxious or depressed, you often retreat from others. You no longer find pleasure in being around people. In the workplace, you may avoid social events and eat lunch at your desk. Unfortunately, this does more harm than good. When you are depressed, the comfort and support of others can be the best medicine.

sleep deprivation

A staggering 37 percent of workers suffer from sleep deprivation.[5] Stress can bring about an imbalance in the body's hormonal system, leading to the release of stimulating hormones such as cortisol. These hormones can cause sleep disturbances. The impact on employees can be significant, resulting in irritability, lost productivity, and increased stress. Sleep impairment is especially harmful to your decision-making skills and causes you to become more easily distracted, less creative, and less able to draw links between information. It also wreaks havoc on your relationships, including relationships at work. Research has found that spouses with fewer sleep problems tend to experience higher levels of happiness. Relationships are also more likely to suffer from romantic conflicts, even when only one partner experiences sleep deprivation! Sleep deprivation has been shown to inhibit your sense of humor since humor requires the high-level cognition that sleep provides us with.

overeating

Stress raises cortisol levels, which in turn, elevate your insulin levels. The insulin causes your blood sugar levels to drop, making you crave sugary, fatty foods. Overeating or consumption of unhealthy foods is an all-too-common response to stress. Jane Jakubczak, a dietitian at the University of Maryland, found that negative emotions are responsible for 75 percent of overeating.[6] The increased anxiety associated with stress commonly leads to mindless eating and a distorted view of how much you've eaten or whether you feel full. Stress can also interfere with your brain's reward system and cause you to crave "comfort foods" such as ice cream or pizza. Overeating also leads to being overweight, which can bring its own health and self-esteem challenges.

drug or alcohol abuse

You've already learned about stress's harmful cognitive effects. When people are stressed, they tend to be more likely to give in to urges and impulses. They often resort to using drugs or alcohol as a coping mechanism, but the effects of this decision can result in long-term harm.

making high-risk decisions

Much like drug or alcohol abuse, high levels of stress can lead to high-risk decision making involving money, sex, or the law. Behaviors that fall into this category include shopping and overspending, compulsive or unsafe sex, stealing, or driving recklessly. The results of these decisions can lead to serious legal or medical problems—or even death.

impulsive or repetitive behaviors

We've already seen that stress can cause obsessive thoughts that lead to anxiety. This obsession also tends to result in impulsive or repetitive behaviors such as gambling, handwashing, counting, magical thinking, and other ritualistic actions. Often there is no rhyme or reason to the behaviors; they simply function as a type of coping mechanism.

Use the following symptom log to reflect on your experiences and assess how you may have experienced or may still be experiencing the more common symptoms of behavioral stress. As you go about your day, jot down your experiences related to each symptom as they occur in Table 1.4 on page 21.

As you can see in Figure 1.5 on page 22, it's important to recognize how stress unfolds and what the warning signs are. Listen to your body.

Symptom	My Experiences	Reflection Questions	My Response
Social withdrawal		How often do you find pleasure around others? How often do you face situations or events that cause you to want to be alone?	
Sleep deprivation		How often do you get 7-9 hours of sleep each night? Do you find it difficult to fall asleep? Stay asleep? Do you suffer from insomnia?	
Overeating		Does your weight fluctuate according to your mood? Are you more likely to gain weight during periods of high stress?	
Drug or alcohol abuse		Have you ever used drugs or alcohol as a coping mechanism against stress? Do you know someone who has?	
Making high-risk decisions involving money, sex, or the law		Have you ever made a risky decision that involves money? What about sex? What about the law? Were these decisions caused by stress?	

TABLE 1.4 **behavioral stress symptom log**

Symptom	My Experiences	Reflection Questions	My Response
Impulsive or repetitive behaviors		Do high levels of stress cause you to engage in impulsive or repetitive behaviors? Which ones? Do they have long-term consequences?	

TABLE 1.4 **behavioral stress symptom log,** continued

Classify the following according to whether they are a cognitive ("C"), emotional ("E"), physical ("P"), or behavioral ("B") effects of stress.

Effect	Cognitive ("C"), Emotional ("E"), Physical ("P"), or Behavioral ("B") Stress Effect
1. Loss of appetite or increased eating	
2. Lack of focus	
3. Upset stomach	
4. Frequent colds	
5. Low sense of self-esteem	
6. Social withdrawal	
7. Low energy	
8. Drinking and using drugs too frequently	
9. Making high-risk decisions involving money, sex, or the law	
10. Impulsive or repetitive behaviors	

Solutions: 1. "B," 2. "C," 3. "P," 4. "P," 5. "E," 6. "B," 7. "P," 8. "B," 9. "B," 10. "B"

FIGURE 1.5 **quiz: what type of stress effect is it?**

good news

Experiencing one of the effects of stress doesn't spell doom and gloom. I have good news! Many of the effects of stress (headaches and irritability, for example) develop before you've officially reached a state of chronic stress. These changes can serve as early signals that you are overly stressed. It's important to heed these warning signs. If you're able to alleviate your stress (with adequate rest and relaxation, for example), your body, mind, and spirit will have a chance to recover. But it's critical to recognize the signs of stress early on, and take action before it manifests as a more serious disease or disorder.

Your success as a leader depends on your ability to recognize stress and take immediate action. Time is of the essence. Prolonging your response will only escalate the negative effects of stress. The key is self-management. You need to take care of yourself before you can take care of your team. Engage in healthy conversations about stress with your team. Encourage them to talk about their stress freely, and teach them to recognize the early signs.

When chronic stress does rear its ugly head, it needs to be taken very seriously. Many of the effects associated with chronic stress can be reversed if they are addressed early enough. Others, however, will cause permanent damage and can be life-threatening. The earlier you confront stress, the better.

a closer look at chronic stress

From now on, when I refer to "stress," you can assume that I am referring to chronic stress. The distinction between acute stress and chronic stress is important (you read about the difference earlier in this chapter). Examples of acute stress include the stress you experience after having an argument with a co-worker, delivering an important presentation, suffering through a bad day at work, or toiling toward a short-term deadline. These events are all short-lived. By contrast, stress, as I am employing it here, is ongoing. It results from the constant stimulation of the body's stress response.

It can sometimes be difficult to differentiate between acute and chronic stress, and in many cases, acute stress turns into chronic stress. The body is well-equipped to cope with acute stress. It can quickly adapt and recover. However, when stress becomes repetitive and prolonged, it takes a major toll on the body. Many of your bodily functions become overworked and may even begin to break down. Take a few minutes to reflect on the following questions:

▶ Do you find yourself getting into a conflict with the same co-worker each day?
▶ Do you face a constant pressure to perform?
▶ Do you perpetually feel inadequately suited for your work?

If you answered "yes" to any of the above, you are likely experiencing chronic stress. As a business leader, your stressors are generally different from those experienced by the general working population. Here are the most common ones, according to the Center for Creative Leadership:[7]

Trying to accomplish more with less than adequate resources in a shorter amount of time. Are you frequently asked to do more with less, and do it faster? Perhaps you've been assigned to open an office in an overseas location but haven't been given a high enough budget or the headcount to do so. Even if you have the necessary resources, you may not have sufficient time. If you work at a publicly traded company, you likely face high pressure to appease shareholders while trying to protect your company's infrastructure and preparing your employees for long-term success. It's impossible to appease all stakeholders at all times. You need to make difficult choices. Buckle up for the ride.

How do you manage this type of stress? It's all about focus. Focusing on the task at hand by planning, organizing, and prioritizing can help. Certain behaviors like defining and clarifying task expectations and sticking to a schedule can also be a godsend. Above all, you must have courage. By giving direct and actionable feedback, managers can help to lower employees' cognitive loads and reduce their stress levels. With increased focus, the stress caused by working on a task can be reduced. Better yet, future stress pertaining to upcoming tasks can be minimized or even eliminated. You have permission to breathe a sigh of relief.

Dealing with the negative aspects of personal relationships. Strong interpersonal relationships are key to a thriving business. Poor relationships between employees have many repercussions. They have been shown to lower job satisfaction and increase stress and depression. In fact, poor employee relations have even been shown to impact customer demand and service. It's all a domino effect. When relationships are weak, projects and initiatives can suffer to the point of jeopardizing the company and its place in the market.

Relationship-building requires skill and constant attention. As Warren Buffett once said, "It takes 20 years to build a reputation and five minutes to ruin it." Relationships between employees can be improved by implementing appropriate forums, training senior management to recognize and deal with conflicts effectively, and hosting or fostering team-building events to improve personal relationships in the workplace.[8]

Competition and lack of teamwork from peers. "Toxic workers" are all too common in the workplace. They come in different forms. Overly competitive co-workers are one variety. They have a strong need to rise to the top and often do so at the expense of others. Is there someone on your team who constantly kisses up to the boss, often at yours' and others' expense? Other toxic workers include free-riders who don't complete their fair share of the workload. In either case, the results can be devastating and lead to high levels of stress. Employees are 54 percent more likely to quit if even one toxic employee joins a team of 20 people.[9]

Poor performance from direct reports. Poor performance is a stressor that affects employees and managers alike. Unfortunately, tackling poor performance is often fairly low on the agenda. So long as employees are following employment law and company protocol, many managers adopt a laissez-faire attitude. The results can be crippling. Poor performance leads to reduced productivity, lower motivation and retention rates, and—you guessed it—stress.

While some performance issues should be dealt with by Human Resources (misconduct or constant absences, for example), most should be addressed by the employee's manager by setting clear expectations, providing sufficient training, and sufficiently motivating their employees.

Unreasonable customers. Managing customer relations is difficult. We've all heard that the customer is king. But customers can easily divert a business's focus and cause undue stress. The most common source of stress from customers is unreasonable demands and expectations. The most effective companies not only meet the needs of customers but exceed them. They focus on the smallest details and create customer-centric cultures. When customer demands are too overbearing, they push back and look for alternative solutions.

conquering chronic stress

Conquering stress requires a multitiered approach. It consists of five steps:

1. *Awareness.* To conquer stress, you must first know what you're up against. Connect the dots between your symptoms and the sources of your stress.
2. *Acknowledgment.* Accept that you are facing stress. In doing so, you must change the way you think about stress by seeing it as a challenge rather than a hardship.
3. *Problem solving.* Create a plan of attack and map out how you will deal with your stress.
4. *Implementation.* Follow through on your plan and take the necessary actions to tackle your stress.
5. *Review.* Stress should be viewed as an opportunity for growth. Reflect on your experiences and determine how to build resilience for the future.

Everyone has a responsibility to address stress. At the personal level, you have a responsibility to take care of yourself and cope with personal, cultural, organizational, and environmental stressors. At the organizational level, companies have a responsibility to take care of their employees. And at the city and government level, entities have a responsibility to take care of their residents and government employees.

Is stress a serious issue for businesses? You probably already know the answer to this question. But just how big is the problem? Research by Harris Interactive has pegged the percentage of stressed workers at 80 percent.[10] Another report by the National Institute for Occupational Safety and Health found that job stress is more strongly linked to health complaints than financial or family problems.[11]

When business leaders are suffering from stress, they are not operating at optimal capacity. Stress impairs leaders' decision-making skills. In his book *The Stress Effect*, Henry Thompson points out that while some "bad decisions can be attributed to inexperience, lack of knowledge, or poor judgment, . . . bad decision-making can also be the result of severe stress on the leader's cognitive and emotional functioning." Remember Piglet from *Winnie-the-Pooh*? Piglet faced perpetually high levels of stress about everything from balloons to beehives to surprises. His high stress levels sapped his energy and caused him to make poor decisions. How often do you feel like Piglet?

Ongoing stress can also lead to burnout. Burnout is a state of mental, emotional, and physical exhaustion. If you're susceptible to burnout, you may feel helpless or overwhelmed. These feelings can affect your work life, home life, and social life.

Poor decision making at the executive level will necessarily affect a company's performance. If enough workers are stressed, it will also affect the bottom line. Productivity will go down, absenteeism and turnover rates will rise, health costs will escalate, and the workplace will be somber and cheerless.

While stress represents a very serious issue for all organizations, the task of addressing and ultimately conquering stress falls on you.

As a leader, you need to take action and attack not only your own stress, but also the stress affecting your employees.

the solutions to stress

Stress is an inevitable component of life, and has a major impact on your well-being. Between 75 and 90 percent of all visits to primary care physicians are directly linked to stress-related problems.[12] As a manager, regardless of your level of seniority, your job brings with it ongoing daily stress. In addition to your everyday duties, you may be called upon to deal with a conflict between your team members, to address a performance issue with an employee, to make a difficult hiring decision, or to confront one of your peers about a personal issue.

But unlike an employee in a non-managerial position, it is hard to get some time away from your stressors. They are ongoing. So what do you do? The solution involves devoting some time each day toward replenishing your mind, emotions, and body. Your stresses are continuous. Your efforts and strategies for dealing with that stress should be similarly continuous and ongoing. The key to success is resilience.

Each individual is different. There is no strict recipe or protocol for dealing with stress. You will need to discover what activities work best for you from the multitude of suggestions and advice in this book. Some remedies are aimed at the individual level, some at the leadership level, others at the organization level, and many at the national and global levels. The ensuing chapters will delve much deeper into the solutions for stress.

managing stress

When you identify that a particular stressor is adversely affecting you or someone else, you now have the wherewithal and resources to correct the stressor. When you zero in on stresses at the company level, you can minimize the specific problems associated with stress and craft a better work environment for all employees, vendors, and customers. These benefits have transformative effects on performance and productivity and necessarily affect the bottom line.

chapter wrap-up

In this chapter, you've started to learn about stress. You've learned that stress is a primal reaction that triggers the fight-or-flight response. You experience stress when you perceive a threat, whether real or imagined, and sense the potential for danger. Stress is highly subjective and differs markedly across individuals.

Stress can be positive, and it can stimulate performance. But there is an inflection point when you begin to lose control and stress manifests in a number of harmful physiological responses. These responses can be cognitive, emotional, physical, or behavioral in nature and have a significant impact on a leader's ability to remain productive, foster healthy relationships, and inspire his or her team.

Stress is a serious issue for businesses and should be top-of-mind. From impaired decision-making to deteriorating relationships to burnout, stress affects a worker's ability to perform and causes the company to miss its targets.

In Chapter 2, you'll start to come to terms with your own stress levels. I've designed an assessment that will allow you to gauge where you stand on the stress spectrum. You'll then be able to pinpoint the best approaches to tackling your stress levels.

your stress
self-assessment

S tress is a global health epidemic. While its effects can single-handedly handicap organizations, stress starts with the
individual. This is because stress is highly subjective. Each
worker experiences the effects of stress differently. If you're
a thicker-skinned worker, you might be able to handle stress
with relative ease. Your colleague, on the other hand, might
find the same stressor unbearable. One stressor might give rise

to headaches in one worker, insomnia in another, and depression in a third. This is because the emotional, cognitive, behavioral, and physical effects of stress depend on many factors, including personal biology, family, and culture of origin as well as access to resources.

Stress can be triggered by a number of factors and, as you learned in Chapter 1, can cause a variety of symptoms. It often creates a negative ripple effect. Consciously or subconsciously, humans are skilled at detecting high levels of stress, and one stressed-out worker in an organization can quickly turn into an epidemic for your business.

understanding where you stand

It's difficult to manage something without knowing how to measure it. By equipping yourself with a mindset and a set of tools that will empower you to recognize and measure stress, you can learn to cope with and, ultimately, combat stress. Because responses to stress are highly individualistic, the most effective mindset and tools will differ between you and the next person to pick up this book. What causes one person enormous—even crippling stress—may be for someone else no more than a blip on the radar.

Any attempt to effectively manage stress must begin with an honest and comprehensive assessment of how you react to stress. Only with an earnest understanding of your proclivity to stress can you develop a targeted approach that will enable you to cope with stress and even squash it in its tracks.

First, you need to draw a clear distinction between individual stress and occupational stress that you experience as a result of your work. Any comprehensive discussion of stress must address the stressors lurking within the workplace. After all, most people spend most of their waking hours at work. According to the American Psychological Association (APA), 65 percent of U.S. employees say their work is a significant source of stress, while more than one-third suffer from chronic work stress.[1] Tight deadlines, long hours, intense work demands, unsupportive or even toxic co-workers, an impaired managerial relationship, fears about job security, and even lack of advancement opportunities all affect stress levels.

Because work plays such a fundamental role in your life, it's critical to evaluate the ways in which your workplace may make you more or less susceptible to stress. In working with my clients, I searched in vain for a tool that would allow them to effectively measure their own stress both at work and at home. A few studies have assessed stress at a holistic level. But to the best of my knowledge, no validated instrument accounts for both individual and workplace stress. If you are interested in my research, please read on. If not, you can skip directly to the worksheet I designed for you, which can be found in Figure 2.1 on page 34.

designing a stress assessment

Recognizing that stress affects individuals in diverse ways, I first reviewed the stress scales that have been devised to help people assess their levels of stress relative to the population at large. The Perceived Stress Scale (PSS), for example, is commonly used to assess individual stress levels. It was developed in 1983 and remains heavily employed. The questions in the PSS ask people to reflect on how often they've felt or thought a certain way during the past month. (For example, "In the last month, how often have you felt that things were going your way?") As its name implies, its objective is to help individuals assess their perceptions of their stress.

Another widely used assessment is the Holmes and Rahe Stress Scale based on the work of psychiatrists Thomas Holmes and Richard Rahe, who, in 1967, began to study whether stress contributes to illness. The scale is a list of 43 stressful life events that, according to Holmes and Rahe's research, can contribute to illness. Each event, called a Life Change Unit (LCU), has a different "weight" (death of a spouse is weighted the highest). After completing the survey, individuals are asked to tally how many LCUs they've experienced in the past year to obtain an estimate of how stress is impacting their health.

I also reviewed several assessments that aim to measure organizational triggers of stress. The Marlin Company and The American Institute of Stress, for example, have devised The Workplace Stress Scale to help individuals assess their levels of job stress as compared to the American work force.

introducing your stress assessment

Using some of these classic exemplars as inspiration, I designed an assessment that accounts for both individual and workplace stresses. After reviewing a host of different stress instruments, I kept track of different survey question themes.

In terms of personal stress, many questions address the physical and emotional manifestations of stress. Some questions addressed mechanisms for coping with stress (regular exercise and a healthy diet, for example).

In terms of workplace stress, some questions ask about co-workers and managers. Some questions ask about the physical workplace environment. Others ask about advancement opportunities.

I consider the assessment below a blend of all the major themes of the existing available instruments. It is holistic and teases apart stress from numerous angles, ensuring that no one topic is over-indexed. As it is not validated, it is intended to provoke insight and discussion, not to diagnose in a clinical manner.

Start your assessment by completing Sections 1 and 2 of the worksheet in Figure 2.1.

Section 1 Instructions

Thinking about your current day-to-day life outside the workplace, respond to each of the following 15 questions by putting a cross [x] below the rating that best describes your experiences over the past week. Do not spend more than ten seconds on any one question.

FIGURE 2.1 **self-assessment sections 1 and 2**

Question	Rarely 1	Occasionally 2	Often 3
1. I experience one or more of the emotional effects of stress described in Chapter 1, including irritability, lack of motivation, a sense of helplessness, and depression.			
2. I experience one or more of the physical effects of stress described in Chapter 1, including muscle tension, headaches, migraines, and digestive problems.			
3. I find myself trying to accomplish more without adequate resources in a shorter length of time.			
4. I am told I engage in Type A behaviors, including competitiveness, aggression, and impatience.			
5. I struggle to get 30 or more minutes of exercise each day.			
6. I struggle to get 7-9 hours of sleep each night and/or have difficulty falling or staying asleep.			
7. I struggle to eat a nutritious, well-balanced diet and find myself under or overeating.			
8. I feel isolated and don't engage in social activities with others outside the workplace.			
9. My routine doesn't include a mindfulness or meditation practice.			
10. I lack confidence in my ability to control my emotions in difficult situations.			
11. When I experience a stressful event, I react immediately before thinking carefully about the situation.			

FIGURE 2.1 **self-assessment sections 1 and 2,** continued

Question	Rarely 1	Occasionally 2	Often 3
12. I feel my life lacks strong purpose.			
13. I think about a significant negative event that has happened to me in the past 6 months (e.g., a death, divorce, adverse health change).			
14. I suffer from burnout, anxiety, or depression.			
15. I find I have too much on my plate and feel overwhelmed by what I need to accomplish.			
Total Score: /45			

Section 2 Instructions

Thinking about your current day-to-day life at work, respond to each of the following 15 questions by putting a cross [x] below the rating that best describes your experiences over the past week. Do not spend more than ten seconds on any one question.

Question	Rarely 1	Occasionally 2	Often 3
1. I struggle to enjoy the company of my co-workers.			
2. I find I have too much on my plate and feel overwhelmed by what I need to accomplish.			
3. I check my work email outside of working hours.			
4. I don't think my boss (or loved one, if self-employed) is supportive of my professional growth.			

FIGURE 2.1 **self-assessment sections 1 and 2,** continued

Question	Rarely 1	Occasionally 2	Often 3
5. I feel my workplace conditions are unsafe.			
6. I find myself working against unreasonable deadlines.			
7. I'm unable to bring my true self to work.			
8. I feel that my work interferes with my personal life.			
9. I don't think I receive appropriate recognition or rewards for my work.			
10. I am rarely given opportunities to learn new skills.			
11. I don't feel my job is secure.			
12. I wish I had a different job.			
13. I rarely take breaks and vacations when I think I need them.			
14. When I wake up, I rarely look forward to going to work.			
15. I find it challenging to concentrate on my work.			
Total Score: /45			

Tally up your score in each of the two sections. Each section is evaluated out of a score of 45. Your total score will be a score out of 90.

Interpreting Your Score

30-49: If your total score in both sections is between 30 and 49, you have a relatively low susceptibility to stress. This does not mean you don't experience stress. It merely means that, whether through nature or nurture, you have developed a stronger barrier to stress than most people. To maximize your personal and professional well-being, you still need to be aware of your stressors, especially those that have a strong impact on you.

FIGURE 2.1 **self-assessment sections 1 and 2,** continued

50-69: If your total score is between 50 and 69, you are moderately prone to stress. You've developed some coping mechanisms but still find yourself negatively affected by stress sometimes. There are many opportunities for you to improve your ability to cope, combat, and even prevent stress.

70-90: If your total score is between 70 and 90, you are highly prone to stress. You frequently encounter situations you deem stressful. You've developed a few coping mechanisms to ward off stress, but they aren't having sufficient impact. You are often impacted by stress's negative effects. Fear not. This realization should be a liberating wake-up call for you.

FIGURE 2.1 **self-assessment sections 1 and 2,** continued

factors that determine how you respond to stress

Now that you've completed some granular self-assessment, it's time to think about some other characteristics of your personality that may determine how you handle stress. From your personality "type" to your gender, there are many factors that play into your relationship with stress. Recognizing those is also part of your self-assessment.

Imagine the following situation. You've been waiting in line for your morning beverage for nearly 20 minutes. At this rate, you are going to be late for an important work presentation. Suddenly, the cashier decides to go on a break. You shoot him a cold glare, which doesn't seem to faze him in the least. You're infuriated. Your pulse escalates, your palms begin to sweat, and you feel a slight headache coming on. Meanwhile, the person behind you in line, who has been waiting nearly as long as you have, and who is also juggling two rambunctious children, seems unflustered. She simply moves to another cashier.

Why are humans so different in their responses to stress? Some of us feel energized, some feel drained, some work harder, and some resort to harmful activities, such as illicit drugs or gambling. To say that stress is a complex phenomenon is an understatement. There are many different variables impacting how you respond to different stresses.

personality

Stress and personality are closely intertwined. Several of the Big Five personality traits (openness, conscientiousness, extroversion/introversion, agreeableness, and neuroticism) have been shown to impact stress levels. One of the most frequently drawn relationships is that between high levels of stress and "Type A" personality types. The Type A-Type B personality hypothesis outlines two distinct personality types. Type A is typically associated with ambitious, competitive, and sometimes aggressive behaviors. Type A individuals also tend to exhibit high levels of impatience and time urgency. They are apt to get frustrated while waiting in line and may walk or talk at a fast pace. They typically yearn for more hours in their day. They also have a strong need to achieve. Research has shown that Type A individuals tend to display several distinct stress-related physical characteristics, including facial tension (such as a clenched jaw) and teeth grinding.

On the flip side, Type B people are typically associated with more relaxed behavior. They rarely fret. Unlike Type A individuals, they don't tend to be overly competitive and don't feel a strong need to be in control of groups or situations. They take each day as it comes. Their more laid-back personality makes them generally less prone to stress. When they *are* subjected to stress, they tend to be highly productive.

While Type A personalities tend to be more susceptible to stress, everyone falls on a continuum. No one is completely Type A or entirely Type B. Additionally, a person can exhibit Type A behaviors in certain circumstances and Type B in others.

And remember, although each person falls in a different spot on the Type A-Type B spectrum, everyone has control over their actions. When it comes to time and anticipatory stress, you are the scribe of your own destiny. Choosing how you think about the events and situations that come your way can change the way you feel about them. Try the quiz in Figure 2.2 on page 40 to see if you're a Type A personality.

Even your level of introversion or extroversion impacts how you respond to stress. Extroverts, for example, are more social and

Answer each of the questions in the following chart to better understand your Type A tendencies.

Reflection	Yes ("Y") or No ("N")
Do you frequently try to multitask and find it difficult to focus?	
When engaging in games or sports, are you significantly more likely to enjoy the activity if you are winning?	
Do you have a strong need to finish things you start?	
Do you frequently find yourself in a state of panic or worry?	
Do you like to set your own deadlines?	

If you answered "yes" to two or more of the above questions, you're likely to skew toward the Type A end of the spectrum and may be more susceptible to stress.

FIGURE 2.2 **quiz: type a personality assessment**

communicative than introverts. As a result, they are more likely to voice their concerns, troubles, and grievances, rather than let them fester internally. This can be immensely powerful in warding off stress.

Additionally, extroverts tend to have more expansive social support systems than introverts. These support systems can also function as powerful shields against stress. Social contact has been shown to boost the production of neurochemicals and the release of endorphins and other "feel-good" hormones. Thus, it's not all that surprising that extroverts have been found to be more optimistic and less likely to experience stress.

Introverts, on the other hand, are much more likely to keep their emotions and thoughts to themselves. They are also less likely to seek out the company of others, which can deprive them of stress-quelling endorphins. While extroverts tend to reap energy from the company of others, introverts tend to gain energy from time alone or one-on-one with a friend. This is in no way a reflection of social skills. On the whole, introverts and extroverts have equally strong social skills. But it can cause introverts to experience higher levels of stress.

Introverts also handle stress very differently from extroverts. Extroverts tend to talk about stress with others, processing their feelings aloud and seeking understanding and comfort from the people they know. Introverts, on the other hand, tend to withdraw when they are stressed. They need space to recharge and come to terms with their situation.

In coping with stress, introverts often find mindfulness, meditation, and other quiet practices rejuvenating. Many introverts also find poetry and journaling enormously beneficial as they tend to prefer to communicate in writing rather than verbally.

Do you consider yourself an introvert or an extrovert? While everyone falls along a spectrum, your level of introversion or extroversion profoundly impacts how likely you are to experience stress.

gender

Author John Gray claimed men are from Mars and women are from Venus. When it comes to stress, it turns out this adage has *some* truth to it. If you're female, you're genetically predisposed to experience higher levels of stress. A 2016 study in *Brain and Behavior* found that women are twice as likely to suffer from severe stress and anxiety as men.[2] If you're a woman, this news should not be alarming but liberating. With an increased understanding of your own vulnerabilities, you'll be better able to develop resilience against stress.

Several bodies of research show that men and women differ markedly in their responses to stress. Part of the difference relates to hormone levels. Women's higher estrogen levels, for example, mean they are more likely to develop depression in response to stressful events. Research by the American Psychological Association has shown that women are more likely than men to report having a significant level of stress.[3] Women are also more likely to report experiencing the physical symptoms associated with stress that we discussed in Chapter 1—specifically headaches, upset stomachs, and indigestion. At the same time, women are less likely to externalize their reactions to stress. In response to stress, women are likely to "tend and befriend" (protecting their offspring and seeking the protection of a group), while men are more likely to go into "fight-or-flight" mode, acting, often rashly, on their stress. Looking at your own situation, does this hold true for you?

wellness habits and routines

Everyone has a wellness routine. For some people, it is well-developed. It includes exercise, a well-balanced diet, meditation sessions, and spiritual practices. For others, it entails little more than a daily shower and brushing their teeth (it's a good week if they go for a jog). Research (and scores of anecdotal evidence) shows that individuals who embrace wellness-promoting habits develop higher levels of resilience against stress.

Decades of research has revealed that exercise is a powerful antidote for stress. Physical activity increases the production of endorphins in the brain. Endorphins function as analgesics, lessening your perception of pain. They give rise to a feeling similar to that triggered by morphine but without the addictive aftereffects.

Exercise also improves the quality of sleep, which is another powerful antidote for stress. A minimum of seven to nine hours of sleep is required to allow the body to rejuvenate. A regular sleep schedule improves concentration and mental clarity and helps regulate mood. In fact, research shows that sleep deprivation causes individuals to react more impulsively and sensitively to negative stimuli. We'll learn much more about the relationship between stress and sleep later in this book.

If your daily regimen is void of healthy food choices, exercise, mindfulness, and other wellness activities, you're more likely to experience higher levels of stress. Again, this should be empowering for you. There are countless activities you can incorporate into your life to develop stronger barriers against stress. And always bear in mind that while it's important to have a routine, it's also important to not feel trapped by it. You can always change it up.

environment

Ever since prehistoric times, humans have been sensitive to their environment. People have a keen awareness of their surroundings, responding to even the most minor environmental changes. It shouldn't come as any surprise, therefore, that your environment has a profound impact on your stress levels.

Your environment includes your physical environment (the neighborhood you live in, for example) and your social environment (your friendship circle, your family, and your loved ones, for example). Many aspects of your physical environment can impact your stress levels. Noise, pollution, traffic, exposure to nature, access to health care and other wellness services and facilities, and the degree of "walkability" have all been shown to affect stress levels. Additionally, your social environment has a significant and enduring impact on your susceptibility to stress. Positive social interactions with friends, family, and significant others can help give meaning and purpose to your life and, in turn, serve as a guard against stress.

In addition to your physical and social environment, your economic environment impacts your stress levels. While, understandably, many individuals report that they worry about not making enough money, research indicates that, barring poverty, a higher level of income is actually associated with higher levels of stress! One 2018 study by LinkedIn that surveyed its U.S. members found that a staggering 70 percent of individuals who bring home an income of $200,000 or more feel stressed at work.[4] However, because so little has been properly researched about stress specifically at work, we should take these pieces of information with a grain of salt.

When considering how your environment impacts your stress levels, take into account the duration of exposure. As will be a common theme throughout this book, stress comes in many forms. It can be a singular event or cumulative in nature. It's much easier to bounce back from one short-term stressor (a parking or jaywalking ticket, for example) than from a long-term stressor (a volatile relationship with a significant other). The more the stressor is repeated and becomes chronic, and the more stressors that are in play, the more difficult it becomes to stay resilient.

where do you go from here?

Go back to the assessment questions in Figure 2.1 and review your results. Read each one carefully, and reflect on your score. Focus on the questions that you answered with a "2" or "3" rating. A careful evaluation will help you develop a more targeted understanding that will help you zero in on the parts of this book that will be most relevant and impactful for you. The following chapters look at stress from many vantage points. Finally, after you have read each chapter of this book, go back and review your survey results again. Reflect on what insights you can apply to your own life that might change your survey results in the future.

Stress is inevitable. It is used to describe the seemingly trivial decision of where to go for dinner, and it is also used to describe the death of a loved one. Everyone has a different perspective on stress. The differences relate to intrinsic factors, including personalities, attitudes, nutritional status, gender, emotional well-being, and wellness.

They also relate to external factors, including differences in physical environment, workplace conditions, personal and professional relationships, and significant life events. Often through no fault of their own, some people are more susceptible to stress than others. Even if you are one of them, this does not mean you are doomed. Accept it, embrace it, and commit to increasing your resilience to stress and living a stress-less life.

chapter wrap-up

In this chapter, you've come to terms with where you fall on the stress spectrum. This should be empowering and liberating. Regardless of where you stand, you now have a much better understanding of what you need to do to combat your stress levels. Consider yourself fortunate. Most individuals don't have the level of insight that reaches further than swatting at symptoms. They rarely have a deep motivation to change.

Now it's time to think about yourself as a leader. Business and leadership are rife with stress. It often materializes during times of change. Many organizations that face near-death experiences struggle with high levels of stress in the aftermath. In Chapter 3, you'll start to pinpoint the specific ways you can decrease your susceptibility to stress.

a holistic approach to stress management

n my work as an executive coach, my engagements with my clients almost always include creating individual development plans (IDPs). They are used to build a specific competency such as emotional intelligence (also known as EQ) or strategic ability. The goal is to identify specific behaviors that can help develop these competencies.[1] IDPs are usually heavily based on 360-degree assessments. A *360-degree assessment* is a process of obtaining feedback from an employee's direct reports, colleagues, and supervisors as well as a self-evaluation by the employee. It can be a great resource to begin to assess your stress levels.

To understand how leaders differ in terms of their individual competencies, I've devised four IDPs loosely based on 360-degree and the Complete Assessment Profiles© of four of my clients who are all grappling with high levels of stress. As you read through each one, reflect on how strongly they resonate with your own tendencies.

anita

Anita was certainly no stranger to success. She had held senior marketing roles at several large technology companies and was heavily recruited to join her current company as its first chief marketing officer. She often organized company-wide events, such as holiday parties and happy hours.

Despite her strong track record of success, Anita had started to doubt herself and her abilities. Never before had she experienced a situation like this. For the first time in her life, Anita wasn't hitting her marketing targets. The conversion rate between marketing qualified leads (MQLs) and sales qualified leads (SQLs), a key indicator of marketing effectiveness, had plummeted by 20 percent over the past quarter.

Overcome with anxiety, Anita felt a sense of hopelessness. She feared her company's situation was spiraling out of control. This constant sense of unease had caused hyperactive tendencies. Anita's direct reports agreed that her decisions and actions often changed with little rhyme or reason.

Despite being overburdened and suffering from a great deal of anxiety, Anita was able to reflect on the current situation with a lot of clarity and perspective. Rather than bottling up her emotions, she was transparent when talking with her supervisor. She spoke passionately about her ambitions to advance to the CEO position. Although these ambitions had since waned, Anita had many of the makings of a successful CEO. She had a strong understanding of how her company's various divisions and functions should work together.

Anita was in her late 40s. She lived with her second husband, and each had a grown child in college. At almost 5'10", she was striking and carried herself like a leader. Her husband was concerned about her well-being and recommended that she see a psychologist. Anita agreed but reluctantly. She considered it a needless distraction from the piles of work she had to contend with.

After three sessions, Anita's psychologist suggested she get a medical evaluation, a full blood panel, and a metabolic workup. She hadn't seen her primary care physician in years. After her test results came back, it was clear that Anita's high levels of stress had resulted in Addison's disease, which is characterized by adrenal deficiency. The good news was that the situation was reversible. But Anita would need to take action fast. Her adrenals were in jeopardy of being depleted.

To make matters worse, Anita's escalated levels of stress had affected her liver and kidneys, the critical bodily organs that process the byproducts of stress. Anita's own mother had died prematurely of kidney disease while they still lived in Mexico, where Anita was born. Her death had led to the family losing their farm. In honor of her mother, Anita was committed to conquering her health issues. This was a wake-up call for her. She knew she could pull through this with her strong family support.

Anita's profile revealed a mature, highly intelligent leader. She had an ease with language and words. She was slightly introverted, but not to the point where she seemed aloof. She had a strong need to be included and inclusive. She was drawn to philosophy as well as the arts. Anita was a woman of high values and integrity. She had a bias toward compromise and collaboration, with a slight aversion to conflict.

As Anita and I discussed the assessments, she talked about her various interests. She told me how she met her husband at an art show. He was a well-known local artist who had been funded by the city to design murals, both in downtown San Francisco and in a couple of impoverished neighborhoods.

During the 360-degree review process, Anita's team members, boss, and colleagues emphasized how much they respected her sharp intellect, expert knowledge of the industry, and great sense of perspective and humor. Each of them commented on how fond they were of her.

It was touching. The ability to connect with others in the work environment and "rally the troops" was a key aspect of Anita's character. It's also a key leadership quality. While many experts are promoted due to their technical abilities, true leaders know instinctively how to connect and engage people individually and in communities.

Anita was pleasantly surprised at how detailed and comprehensive the assessment was. She enjoyed reflecting on her strengths and capabilities. The areas where she needed improvement were no surprise, although they still stung a little.

Based on a set of psychological, business, and 360-degree reviews, I identified three core competencies for Anita to focus on over the coming weeks and months:

1. *Career ambition.* Anita had started to severely doubt her abilities as a leader. While she once had high hopes of one day taking over as CEO, she now viewed this as a mere fantasy. In order to advance in the corporate ranks, Anita would need to regain her career ambition and better articulate her value and worth to her company's senior leadership and board members.

    Anita freely admitted that she'd lost some of her ambition and hoped to regain it. Her lack of career ambition is all too common among stressed leaders.

2. *Priority setting.* Anita had always wanted to do it all. Early in her career, this strategy worked well for her. She felt like Wonder Woman and took on more and more responsibility over time. But as Marshall Goldsmith said, what got you here won't get you there. A prototypical firstborn child, Anita was a perfectionist. She had a hard time saying "no," which caused her to overcommit herself in a crisis environment. She

struggled to prioritize her time, which increased the stress on her team members. If you've ever transitioned from midlevel to executive leadership, then you probably know that it often causes highly ambitious employees to agree to too much too soon.

3. *Timely decision making.* Anita's 360-degree review revealed that she had become more fickle over the past few weeks. Several of her direct reports commented that she seemed "flip-floppy," changing course frequently. Anita's uncertainty slowed her decision making, creating a lot of unrest among her team members. They lacked direction and didn't know where to focus their efforts. She was a little shocked to hear this, although she had sensed it herself. It wasn't that she was trying to stall, flip-flop, or avoid. It was that she couldn't seem to think clearly enough to make timely decisions.

Together, Anita and I reviewed the long list of stress side effects, which included lack of clarity of thought. Stress clouds judgment and often results in poor decision making. Anita agreed that these were the key competencies she needed to work on and that she would benefit from my coaching. She was looking forward to acting as the leader of the stress team and hoped it would be good practice for the future.

personal reflection: anita

Here are a few questions for you to ponder as you think about Anita's story. We'll do this for each case study in this chapter.

▶ Are you similar to Anita in any way?

▶ Does Anita remind you of a colleague?

▶ How do you prioritize your work and your time?

▶ How do you make and communicate decisions? Have you asked for feedback in this area?

▶ Have you ever felt your career ambitions deteriorate? Was it in response to stress?

▶ Do you have trouble saying "no" to requests and demands?

tim

Tim had been very successful in his operations position so far. He had a unique ability to be creative, connect dots across the company where he worked, and implement his ideas at the operational level. He had put processes in place that had fueled his company's growth and made internal processes more efficient. For instance, when launching his company's customer relationship management (CRM) system to customers, he immediately saw the need to implement it internally as well. His company was quick to adopt the software, and to much success.

Tim had always been driven by a competitive fire. He had been a competitive swimmer in college, narrowly missing a berth to compete in the 1996 Olympics. When he joined his company four years ago, he brought that competitive spirit with him. Three years later, he was promoted to director of operations, a midlevel position reporting to the COO.

But recently, Tim's competitive spirit had waned. His fight-or-flight response to stress had caused him to freeze. The stress of his current environment had left him with a pessimistic outlook on life. Since his divorce two years ago, work had been his only reprieve.

Now he felt anxious and depressed. He had experienced two panic attacks in recent months, and the latest episode prompted him to drop out of an upcoming Iron Man competition for which he had been training for almost 18 months. Physically, his bodily processes had deteriorated. He moved and thought more slowly than he used to.

Tim had started to avoid all social engagements, partially out of fear of having another anxiety attack. Even the simplest challenges seemed insurmountable. He sometimes felt like he was being judged and had trouble concentrating for more than a short time. All this had impacted his work. His peers described him as just going through the motions at times.

Last week, during a team meeting, Tim's boss asked for volunteers to join a task force to evaluate his company's pricing strategy. On paper, it was a great opportunity. The task force was extremely high-profile, and his boss told him the team really needed his expertise. But Tim had little interest in joining. In the past, Tim would stand his ground and voice his opinions in meetings. He used to love to pontificate, to imagine new business models and markets, and to think out loud. Now he was hesitant to give his opinions, especially if they were at odds with the majority.

Tim was in his early 40s and had been raised in the Ukraine. His main emotional connection was with his cat, Scruffles, who was a gift from a colleague. He was medium height with an athletic build and a shaved head. He sometimes felt sad, helpless, and hopeless. He had noticed changes in his appetite, not feeling as hungry as he used to. He had trouble concentrating, even being unable to watch an entire episode of *Game of Thrones*, one of his favorite TV shows.

Tim's negative mental state worried him, so he decided to look into his situation. After hours of research, Tim, in a typically analytical way, concluded that his prefrontal cortex was likely affected by his constantly high stress levels. Although depression affects multiple parts of the brain, it has an especially strong impact on the prefrontal cortex. Tim told me about his research, and I confirmed that it was backed by credible sources.

People tend to forget that their feelings don't come out of the blue; there are physiological causes for them. Most people are not psychologists, physicians, or even biology majors, so this way of discussing feelings might seem strange. But talking about it in clinical terms was useful to Tim.

Individuals who experience depression typically have a left prefrontal cortex that shows signs of decline and weakness. While the left half of the prefrontal cortex is responsible for producing positive feelings, the right half is responsible for producing negative feelings. Was Tim experiencing right prefrontal cortex impairment or left prefrontal cortex impairment?

I did some additional research and gave Tim some literature. He found it very interesting. Tim learned that his anxiety had likely been caused by escalated activity in the basal ganglia. Located under the cortex of the brain, the *basal ganglia* are a concentrated group of neurons that drive motivation. When you have a healthy supply of dopamine in the basal ganglia, your energy levels are high and you have a strong sense of motivation. Individuals with anxiety disorders often experience increased basal ganglia activity.

Tim felt horrified but, at the same time, comforted by what he learned. Somehow having a biological explanation for his feelings allowed him to accept what was going on with his mood and mind. He started to see a clear link between biology and leadership and he began to see how he needed to make some changes.

Tim's profile also revealed an introverted, conceptual thinker. He was highly creative and imaginative with a strong interest in philosophy, music, and social causes. He was detail-oriented, with a very high IQ. Tim didn't like the ambiguities in leadership, team dynamics, and implementation. He preferred an open-ended approach to projects and relationships and needed things to be mapped out, step by step.

This was very much at odds with the realities of the business world—especially a company coming out of the red. Yet many people are like Tim, even when they are not under stress.

Tim's 360-degree review revealed that some people were concerned about the changes in his behavior over the past few months. He was closed off, "like a brick wall," one of his peers said. Some of his team members also noted that he lacked compassion. "He cares more about his cat than about us," another review read. Tim felt disheartened by his reviews. As he read through them, he felt a wrench in his stomach. "It's like a divorce all over again," he thought. I tried to point out that his reviews showed a balance between his strengths and areas of opportunity.

I recommended he focus on three core competencies in his journey ahead. We reviewed the basic concepts and worked together to establish the competencies that Tim felt excited to work toward. We determined Tim's three areas of focus should be:

1. *Dealing with ambiguity*. After some personal and professional issues had stressed him out to the nth degree, Tim had faced all the ambiguity he could handle. He felt paralyzed, no longer

able to cope with change. Any sense of risk or uncertainty put him on edge. He needed to learn to better manage ambiguity and shift gears comfortably during uncertain times. This would make him more patient and improve his interpersonal relationships, and it would benefit him in the long term for a job as a COO. The ability to manage ambiguity is critical in today's world where business dynamics and markets are in constant flux. Research has shown that successful leaders must be able to navigate ambiguous waters.[2]

2. *Approachability.* Tim had put up an iron wall between himself and his colleagues. He had become aloof. He needed to focus on rebuilding rapport with his co-workers, improving his listening skills, and demonstrating compassion. It was not in his nature to be closed off. After being told this, Tim actually started to look forward to being part of the team again.

3. *Composure.* Several of Tim's 360-degree reviews revealed that he is a pressure cooker. He's easily knocked off-balance by unexpected events. He can quickly become defensive and irritable when faced with conflict and disagreement.

After rereading my report, Tim felt a bit hurt by some of the comments. He knew that some of the feelings were caused by misunderstandings, but it was hard to see it in writing. Tim had visceral reactions to stress, many of which were at odds with his true nature. A keen sense of awareness is critical to leadership. Leaders must gain the trust of their team members and establish a healthy culture. Above all, they must avoid spreading doubt and panic.

personal reflection: tim

Think about Tim's acceptance of and reactions to stress. Are you similar to Tim in any way? Ask yourself:

▸ Does Tim remind you of a colleague?
▸ Have you felt overwhelmed or depressed?
▸ Have you ever felt your competitiveness wane? Was it in response to stress?

> Do you uncharacteristically have trouble wanting to connect with people?
> Do you consider yourself good at dealing with ambiguity?
> Are there times when you feel like a pressure cooker?

madison

Madison was promoted to director of HR immediately before the economic downturn. She had been hired as a human resources coordinator, a position that involved managing paperwork, not people. Her first task had been to rewrite the existing job candidate offer. She scrapped it entirely, replacing the cold, legalistic jargon with warm and inviting language. She had also replaced the long saga about the company's history with a description of their employee benefits.

Madison's promotion left her tasked with managing a team of 12 people, something she had never done before. This promotion, while welcomed, was the main source of stress for Madison. She wanted to avoid ruling with an iron fist, but she went too far, becoming more of a friend to her team than a leader. Madison's boss, the chief people officer, had received several complaints from her direct reports about her lack of managerial experience, which stressed Madison even more.

After too many sleepless nights, Madison decided to enroll in a sleep clinic and was diagnosed with moderate insomnia. The sleep specialist noted that she suffered from extremely elevated levels of cortisol, one of the stress hormones.

An individual's circadian rhythm is defined by his or her levels of cortisol. When everything is functioning properly, your cortisol levels rise in the morning, giving you the energy you need for the day, and gradually decline, reaching a low point in the evening. When your cortisol levels are imbalanced, it can trigger sleep disruption. That's what was happening to Madison. She increasingly found herself tossing and turning in bed at night. In the morning, she yawned frequently and was often forgetful. She had forgotten her keys three times in the past month.

Madison's acupuncturist and primary care physician both tried to help her with hypertension, which had worsened because of weight gain. They were concerned about her weight gain and insomnia. Frequent sessions with her acupuncturist allowed Madison to go on with her life. But they were short-term fixes. She still hadn't overcome her conditions. She started taking blood pressure medications to help maintain healthy blood pressure levels. Madison was determined to get to the root cause of all this. Her dad had died of a heart attack when she was 20. Although she had always been an independent spirit, she had been very close to her dad and stepmom and felt the loss tremendously.

As I spoke with Madison, I was touched by her description of her life. Madison had enjoyed the dating scene in the past and had always cherished close friendships. Yet lately, she had been too tired to go on dates or out with friends after work. Her relationships with her friends had deteriorated. Even her high school friends had told her they were tired of being sounding boards for her troubles. Madison had resorted to binge-watching Netflix in the evenings and often found herself eating throughout the episodes.

Madison's profile revealed an extroverted systems thinker. She was inclusive in groups and loved to initiate close friendships and rituals. She had a reputation for going all out when celebrating Halloween and the Fourth of July. Madison was born in the Avenues in San Francisco and had graduated from a city college with a degree in mathematics. She was a logical and practical thinker with a high IQ. She loved building models. Recently she had become fascinated by models for culture change and employee engagement and was considering developing an online course on those subjects. She had a voracious appetite for learning, devouring leadership books, especially on the science of leadership.

Madison's 360-degree reviews revealed that she was well-liked. Her peers respected her caring and compassionate tendencies. "Our office mom," read one review. "Like a cuddly teddy bear," said another. However, while her reviews were mostly heartfelt, there were a few, particularly from her direct reports, that expressed concerns about Madison's lack of managerial experience.

Based on her profiles and 360 data, I recommended that Madison focus on developing three core competencies in the weeks ahead. She immediately agreed and mentioned liking the structure of these competencies:

1. *Delegating.* Madison grew up in a single-parent household until her mom married when she was 16. She had few people to rely on and was often left to fend for herself. Delegating had always been a bit of a foreign concept to Madison, but to succeed in her new managerial position, she needed to learn to share her responsibilities by delegating and holding her direct reports accountable.

2. *Developing direct reports.* Madison's emotional tendencies have caused her to act more as a friend than a manager to her direct reports. She needed to do a better job at setting her direct reports up for success. She needed to become a people builder and help her team advance toward their own career goals and aspirations. The benefits of developing team members are far greater than the time costs required. A telltale sign of an effective manager is a direct report whose performance shoots up under their watch and, in the end, surpasses the leadership capabilities of previous managers.

3. *Managing vision and purpose.* Madison's lack of managerial and leadership experience was front and center in her 360-degree reviews. Her direct reports appreciated her caring nature but feel lost and unguided at times. Madison needed to do a better job of communicating a compelling vision and a strong sense of purpose for her team. She needed to inspire and motivate her team. When she was uncertain about her team's vision and purpose, she needed to ask for clarification. Thanks to her love of models and conceptual thinking, Madison had a leg up on other first-time managers. She was bound to experience a shorter learning curve.

personal reflection: madison

Think about how Madison approacheed and dealt with stress. Are you similar to Madison in any way? Ask yourself:

▶ Does Madison remind you of a colleague?

▶ Have you ever been a first-time manager? Did you struggle to delegate?

▶ Have you ever worked with a first-time manager who acted more as a friend than a manager?

▶ What effect did it have on you and your work?

▶ How much time do you spend thinking about how to develop your direct reports, and what would they say about that?

li

Li worked in sales at a software as a service (SaaS) company in San Francisco. The economic downturn hit Li and his team hard. Sales numbers plummeted, and customer churn rates increased. Li had been optimistic about the company's future but now expressed serious concerns. He was extremely anxious about his company's longevity and especially about his ability to bring in enough income to support his family and other commitments.

Li's mood had been affected by his stress. At work, his direct reports noted that he was unpredictable. Sometimes he was missing in action. Sometimes he was inclined to micromanage. He was laser-focused on hitting impossible sales targets. His direct reports feared that he was prioritizing short-term gains at the expense of long-term performance. Li was known for offering clients sharp discounts to retain and gain their business, but these steep discounts were eating away at the bottom line. Li's co-workers were also concerned about his tunnel vision. His team was highly enthusiastic about a new predictive technology that had recently hit the market. They were confident it would help them boost lead generation. But Li didn't want to hear it. He was focused on hitting sales numbers and didn't seem to care about the new technology, even if it did promise to enhance sales efficiency.

Li grew up around Clement Street in San Francisco and was in his early 40s. He was married with three children, all under ten years old. Li had been a standout at his company. He started there as Director of North American Sales after a long stint as an account executive at a rival firm, and after crushing his quota for six consecutive quarters, he was promoted to VP of sales.

At home, Li's partner had noted a marked change in his mood and personality. When they met, Li was extremely patient. In the past, he had practiced yoga, meditation, and mindfulness almost daily. Now he was a different man. Li had stopped his mindfulness practices and had become very irritable, frequently snapping at his family. In just the last week before we met Li's youngest son, James, accidentally scraped Li's new car while his older brother was teaching him how to ride a bike. Although the scrape could easily be touched up, Li exploded in anger. He wasn't appeased by James' tears and remorse and fumed about the incident for days.

Li's doctor prescribed an antidepressant, but Li refused to take it. Instead, he turned to alternative medicines and started to eat more healthfully. With the exception of a nagging cold, Li's stress had not yet manifested in any physical symptoms.

I was struck by how well Li handled his stress. Despite suffering from high levels of anxiety about the future of the company and his own job, he was able to talk about his concerns with a lot of clarity. Li explained his views on some key changes that needed to take place at his company to reduce stress. I was impressed. I felt like I was listening to a finely tuned sales pitch. His proposals were extremely tactical, grounded in logic rather than emotion.

Li's profile revealed an extrovert with top-notch organizational skills. He was vigilant about keeping his desk clean and loathed distraction. He had a strong interest in philosophy, religion, and music. His playlist included an eclectic mix of tunes, from Christian rock to calypso and everything in between. Li also had a strong need for closure and shunned multitasking, needing to complete one task before embarking on the next. He was eager to shape his surroundings and preferred a structured and predictable environment.

Li's 360-degree review was mostly positive. His co-workers admired his ability to consistently increase sales. But they also expressed reservations about his tendency to micromanage and the way he treated his direct reports sometimes lashing out at them. Those feelings hadn't yet escalated to the point of resentment, but they were cause for concern.

After reviewing his psychological, business, and 360-degree assessments, Li and I honed in on three core competencies for him to focus on moving forward:

1. *Strategic agility.* Li grew up surrounded by a family of doctors, where medical credentials and certification were viewed as the epitome of success. When he told his parents he was destined for a career in business, he felt as though he had failed them. This looming sense of failure was behind Li's profound need to achieve spectacular short-term, sequential wins. He needed to develop more of a long-term orientation, focusing on and anticipating future trends and consequences.

2. *Managing through systems.* Li's strong focus on short-term gains had also resulted in a tendency to micromanage. He needed to learn to manage from a distance and avoid intervening with his team. He had to learn to manage through systems and even create some new systems specific to his team. All too often, senior managers avoid using the systems at their companies, instead punting work to administrative assistant. But Li was different. He held himself to the same standards as everyone else at his company.

3. *Caring about direct reports.* Li's 360-degree reviews also revealed that his direct reports would like him to be more caring and attentive to their needs. He needed to do a better job of listening to his direct reports' issues, helping them build their skills, and working with them to develop their careers. He had to show an interest in their perspectives and understand the concerns and barriers that exist between them. And he needed to avoid transferring his own stress onto them. Li was caring by nature, but the stress of the past couple of years had worn

on him tremendously. Stress often causes leaders to withdraw and bottle up their emotions rather than express them, which can be toxic. Leaders must first look inward in times of stress. They must determine and come to terms with their emotions, rather than dismiss them.

personal reflection: li

Think about how Li dealt with stress. Are you similar to Li in any way? Ask yourself:

▸ Does Li remind you of a colleague?
▸ Do you have a tendency to micromanage?
▸ Are you more likely to micromanage in times of stress?
▸ How caring would your direct reports rate you on a scale of 1–5?
▸ Do you find yourself prioritizing short-term wins over long-term gains?

your leadership competencies

Like all leaders, you have strengths and weaknesses. A solid understanding of your core competencies can help you gain insight into how and why you might be more susceptible to specific stressors. Do you have an accurate idea of how you are viewed by your colleagues? When was the last time you asked for feedback about your specific skills, personality traits, or management style? What are your strengths, and which areas need improvement? How accurate is that assessment? Use Figure 3.1 on page 63 to rank your core competencies.

Once you know your competencies, you can start to think of stress management in much the same way as your other daily hygiene practices, such as washing your hands, brushing your teeth, and taking a shower. A proactive approach is far more effective at correcting stress in its acute stages before it reaches chronic levels.

To address your stress, embrace a four-pronged strategy: Identify your internal stressors, identify your external stressors, acknowledge your fears, and talk about your stress.

Listed below are the core competencies that the four leaders profiled in this chapter needed to develop. Now let's talk about you: Rank each competency from 1 to 3 (with "1" being the most important and "3" being the least important) according to how important it is for you to develop the competency to become a better leader and/or achieve your career goals.

Competency	Ranking	Explanation (Optional)
Career ambition (Anita)		
Priority setting (Anita)		
Timely decision making (Anita)		
Dealing with ambiguity (Tim)		
Approachability (Tim)		
Composure (Tim)		
Delegating (Madison)		
Developing reports (Madison)		
Managing vision and purpose (Madison)		
Strategic agility (Li)		
Managing through systems (Li)		
Caring about direct reports (Li)		

Focus your efforts on the competencies you ranked "1," "2," and "3" in terms of priority. Don't try to build too many competencies at once. Focus is key.

FIGURE 3.1 quiz: rank your competencies

identify your internal stressors

The first coping mechanism against stress is to identify your own internal stressors. Internal stressors are sources of stress that are triggered from within your body or mind. They frequently stem from your personal goals, expectations, and perceptions. According to experts at HelpGuide.org, common internal stressors include the following:[3]

▸ Pessimism
▸ An inability to accept reality

▶ Negative self-talk

▶ Unrealistic expectations

▶ Rigid thinking, lack of flexibility

▶ An all-or-nothing attitude

▶ A need to always be perfect

Perfectionism is one of the most common internal stressors affecting leaders and executives. If you are a perfectionist, anything less than perfection will push your anxiety button. Ironically, the symptoms of internal stressors can be an additional source of stress. You may worry about your insomnia—how will you manage to deliver your presentation at the early morning board meeting if you can't sleep? These ruminations escalate stress levels to new peaks. As stress rises, it becomes more and more difficult to relax and rejuvenate, making recovery much harder. Needless to say, perfectionism can be unproductive and unpleasant for your team, too. Take the quiz in Figure 3.2 below to see how "perfect" you are.

Think about your own internal stressors relative to the bulleted list above. Do you have certain goals, expectations, standards, or perceptions that make you feel uneasy? Use Table 3.1 on page 65 to list at least five internal stressors that you face. Use a scale of 1 to 10 to indicate how significantly each stressor affects you (with "1"

Reply to the following statements with a yes ("Y") if you agree or a no ("N") if you disagree.

Situation	Yes ("Y") or No ("N")
I'm likely to unnecessarily double- and triple-check an email before I send it.	
I tend to plan my days in advance.	
Minor errors in work bother me.	
When given instructions, I tend to follow them word for word.	

If you responded "Y" to two or more statements, you are likely to exhibit perfectionist tendencies.

FIGURE 3.2 **quiz: are you a perfectionist?**

Internal Stressor	Rating (1-10)

TABLE 3.1 **rating your internal stressors**

indicating hardly at all and "10" indicating an almost paralyzing amount of stress).

identify your external stressors

In addition to internal stressors, you're also faced with external stressors. These stressors are caused by external factors and are often difficult to control. Common external stressors include:

▸ Major career changes, including promotions and terminations
▸ Strained relationships with co-workers and/or supervisors
▸ Poor company performance
▸ Intense workloads
▸ Lack of required resources
▸ Unreasonable customers
▸ Changing market dynamics, including recessions and competitive threats

While the workplace is a ripe breeding ground for many of the external stressors facing leaders, they are also caused by forces outside the workplace. Relationship problems, financial difficulties, or health complications can all cause significant stress.

Internal and external stressors can trigger similar physical and psychological effects. Insomnia, headaches, and irritability, for example, are all commonly associated with both internal and

External Stressor	Rating (1–10)	Real ("R") or Imagined ("I")

TABLE 3.2 **rating your external stressors**

external stressors. As with internal stressors, your most effective weapon against the external stressors that are affecting you is to identify them.

What are your external stressors? Jot them down in Table 3.2. Include the big, the medium, and the small, and use a scale of 1 to 10 to indicate how much each stressor affects you (with "1" indicating hardly at all and "10" indicating an almost paralyzing amount of stress). In the right-hand column, indicate whether each stressor is real or imagined (that is, only occurring in your thoughts and dreams).

acknowledge your fears

Now take some time to list your fears. I call this exercise, "What's the worst that can happen?" It's a technique I learned from my mom. "What's the worst that can happen?" is a system for thriving in high-stress environments. In this exercise, you visualize the worst things that could possibly happen to you. By doing so, you'll become less afraid to take action. The only way to truly conquer your stress is to define and examine your fears.

My mom was a teacher and highly organized. She created the chart in Table 3.3 on page 67 to walk you through this exercise. Think about your biggest fears, the absolute worst situations you can envision unfolding, and complete the following chart:

	Define	Prevent	Visualize	Repair
	What are the worst things that could happen?	How do I prevent each of my fears from happening?	If I don't take action to overcome my fear, what is the cost?	If the worst does happen, how can I fix it?
Fear: I bomb at the presentation.	– People get bored. – I get fired.	– I work with somebody on my presentation. – I perform well at all other aspects of my job.	–I never learn to handle my fear about presentations.	– If people are bored, oh well, I will shorten the presentation and apologize. – If I get fired, I will get another job.
Fear				
Fear				

TABLE 3.3 **what's the worst that can happen?**

talk about your stress

Far too many people avoid sharing their stress with friends or family. They think they are lone wolves, struggling on all by themselves. But family and friends can be important sources of relief and support during times of stress. Your close connections know you and embrace you for who you are. Be open with them about your stress levels.

Many successful leaders also seek professional help to cope with their stress, even when they're surrounded by loved ones or have access to employee assistance programs (EAPs) at work. You should consider seeking peer, group, or professional assistance as well. Don't try to convince yourself that your stress levels aren't that bad. If your stress and anxiety are affecting your day-to-day life, it's a red flag that it's time to seek professional help. A professional will help you find the internal strength to deal with your stress. You'll then be able to move onward and upward.

control your unhealthy behaviors

As you talk about your stress, you may discover that you can identify some unhealthy behaviors related to it. When individuals are shackled by stress, they often resort to unhealthy coping mechanisms, such as abusing prescription or illicit drugs, smoking, emotional eating, self-inflicted harm, gambling, compulsive shopping, or any other activity that promises to ease their pain. There are a number of free resources available to help you address your unhealthy behaviors, including peer support groups and 24-hour help lines. Any of the 12-step programs, such as Narcotics Anonymous, Overeaters Anonymous, or Alcoholics Anonymous (all of which are paths to recovery for addiction, compulsion, and other behavioral issues), can be valuable free resources. Use them. They are there to help you.

Identify three steps in the personal challenge plan in Table 3.4 below that you can take to address your unhealthy behaviors. For

Activity	Purpose	How Will I Commit?
Example: Yoga	Example: To help address emotional eating	Example: Call my local gym and buy a one-month group class in which I will be held accountable.

TABLE 3.4 **personal challenge: your three-step stress plan**

example, if you struggle with emotional eating, you could sign up for yoga classes. Emotional eating is caused when people dissociate their body from their mind. Yoga can help you develop a stronger connection to your inner self and, in doing so, ward off emotional eating. The new activity you choose may feel unfamiliar or uncomfortable at first, but be open to the experience. Embrace it.

immerse yourself

Another coping mechanism you can use to your advantage is to find one or more activities outside work that you can wholly dedicate yourself to. Your chosen immersive activity could be a creative endeavor such as music or art. It could be an existing hobby that you could spend more time on. Whatever it is, it needs to be an activity you enjoy so that it diverts your attention from work. You need total immersion to recover from stress. True resilience comes from successful recovery periods.

Immersive activities fall into two categories: receptive or creative. *Receptive experiences* relieve stress by diverting your attention away from daily stressors. *Creative activities*, on the other hand, help you acquire new skills that can give you a sense of accomplishment. Take the quiz in Figure 3.3 on page 70 to classify them.

The psychological detachment you feel when you participate in immersive activities has been found to protect against exhaustion and health impairment.[4] It's also key for relaxation, which helps regenerate your mental and physical resources. Do you know whether it's better to engage in creative or receptive experiences if you want to experience true relaxation?

If you guessed creative, you're half right. While creative activities have been shown to be more effective at promoting recovery from stress, true relaxation is best accomplished by engaging in a combination of both receptive and creative activities.[5]

What activities do you turn to when you're stressed? Do they divert your attention or escalate your stress levels? Do they require learning new skills? What other activities might you try?

Classify the following activities according to whether they are receptive ("R") or creative ("C") experiences.

Activity	Receptive ("R") or Creative ("C")
1. Watching a movie	
2. Learning to play the guitar	
3. Going shopping	
4. Going on a seven-day cruise	
5. Learning a new language	

Solutions: 1. "R," 2. "C," 3. "R," 4. "R," 5. "C"

FIGURE 3.3 **quiz: receptive vs. creative experiences**

your stress-quelling activity

Choose an activity to completely immerse yourself in for at least the next ten days. Use Table 3.5 on page 71 to track your stress levels (using a scale of 1 to 10) before and after engaging in the activity. Record your answers below.

It's important to wholly commit to the activity. Remove all electronic devices from your reach (unless the activity requires them). Take ten deep breaths, inhaling deeply and then exhaling completely. Don't be afraid to fail, and if you do, celebrate it. Avoid thinking about anything but the activity at hand. Devote your complete attention to the activity for at least 20 minutes. You can do this!

seek support

Many people dealing with stress feel like a lone warrior in their fight. Many say they have no one to rely on for emotional support and are hesitant even to admit they need support, viewing it as a sign of weakness. Leaders and executives are especially reluctant to admit it, believing that toughing it out will lead to success. It won't.

Day	Stress level (1-10) before activity	Stress level (1-10) after activity
Day 1: Walk to work listening to "Bohemian Rhapsody"	6	2
Day 2		
Day 3		
Day 4		
Day 5		
Day 6		
Day 7		
Day 8		
Day 9		
Day 10		

TABLE 3.5 **personal challenge: immersion activity log**

Research has shown that a strong social support network improves your ability to cope with stressful situations and alleviates the effects of emotional distress.[6] It can even enhance your resilience to stress. A study conducted by the APA found that the average overall stress level among people who reported having no emotional support was 6.2 on a 10-point scale, compared with the 4.8 reported by people who said they had adequate emotional support.[7]

The good news is that there are many ways to build your social support network. Consider volunteering at a homeless shelter, enrolling in a pottery class, or registering for a dance class. Embrace the new experiences and the people you'll meet.

identify your support network

Using Table 3.6 on page 72, write down at least six individuals who are part of your support network. Commit to reaching out to each

Support Network Member	How Will I Reach Out?
Aisha and John	Play Euchre

TABLE 3.6 **personal challenge: identify your support network**

one of them within the next two weeks. Schedule a movie date, a board game party, or a baking party for example.

stress vs. burnout

Burnout is a state of mental, emotional, and physical exhaustion that occurs when stress continues for a long time. When you're suffering from burnout, you feel tired and drained. Your immune system is affected, and you are more likely to get sick. You may feel a sense of failure, helplessness, and loneliness. Burnout can cause people to become cynical and negative, lose their motivation, and withdraw from their responsibilities. When you experience stress, you may feel that too much is being demanded of you. When you experience burnout, on the other hand, you likely feel empty and detached. Classify your symptoms in the quiz in Figure 3.4 on page 73.

Once you've taken the quiz, look at your answers. If you answered five or six questions correctly, give yourself a big pat on the back. As you can see from the solutions, stress engages the fight-or-flight reaction, causing us to overreact emotionally and become hyperactive physically. Burnout, on the other hand, causes disengagement, numbed emotions, emotional fatigue, and a sense of hopelessness.

Classify the following symptoms as more characteristic of either stress or burnout.

Symptom	Stress ("S") or Burnout ("B")
1. Feelings of disengagement	
2. Feelings of over-engagement	
3. Loss of physical energy	
4. Loss of motivational and emotional energy	
5. Primarily physical damage	
6. Primarily emotional damage	

Solutions: 1. "B," 2. "S," 3. "S or B," 4. "B," 5. "S," 6. "B"

FIGURE 3.4 **quiz: stress vs. burnout**

How do you treat burnout? Recommended treatments range from taking time off, getting more sleep, learning to set effective boundaries, getting and giving support, and reducing stress as much as possible. A counselor can help guide you through this process.

chapter wrap-up

So far, we've discussed how stress affects different individuals. We've also looked at ways to deal with stress at the personal level. But you must also tackle stress at the company level, which you'll read more about in Chapter 10.

Stress must be tackled at multiple angles. You must identify your internal stresses, such as pessimism and self-talk, and your external stressors, like intense workloads or unreasonable customers. The key to overcoming your fears is acknowledging them. By performing the "What's the worst that can happen?" exercise and visualizing the worst-case scenarios, you'll be less afraid to take action. Don't walk the journey alone. Talk about your stress with friends, family, and members of your community. You can speed the recovery process by immersing yourself in an activity outside work, like learning to play the piano or taking a Karate class.

What's the biggest stressor you face? What is your biggest fear? How can you prevent your biggest fear from coming true? How often do you talk openly about your stress? Do you have a strong support network to turn to? Have you ever felt so stressed that you have felt paralyzed?

Now that you understand the stressors that are gnawing away at you, it's time to develop a game plan. The next section of the book is dedicated to this. You'll develop strategies and tactics to cope with and conquer stress, and you'll learn how to apply these tactics to your day-to-day life.

chapter 4

introducing your
five-finger action plan
to wave away stress

a combination of external and internal factors can generate a lot of stress. Perhaps employees are worried about the survival of their company. They could be anxious that they might eventually be laid off. Confusion about job definitions and tasks can add to that stress.

While going through current research in an effort to better understand how my clients can tackle stress, I became fascinated by the concept of neuroplasticity: the brain's ability to change throughout a person's life. The human brain, although a creature of habit, is immensely powerful. It is flexible and can reorganize itself over time, learning to cope and adapt to challenges. The amount of gray matter can increase, new neural pathways can develop, and existing neural networks can expand.

Much of the research I saw confirmed that stress disrupts neuroplasticity. When neuroplasticity is reduced, the brain becomes more rigid and inflexible, and you become more vulnerable to stress. Fortunately, by changing your habits and developing stress-reducing practices, you can induce neuroplasticity and alter your brain structure to more positively respond to stress. You can literally rewire your brain. Isn't that cool?

This is good news. You can put it to use immediately by playing chess, tinkering away at a Sudoku puzzle, or going for a jog. Studies have shown that a combination of several different types of stress-reducing activities is more effective than a single activity on its own. For example, combining meditation and aerobic exercise reduces stress more effectively than either activity alone.

Why is this relevant? Pointing at stress won't cure it. And wagging your finger at yourself to stop stressing won't motivate you for long. To truly wave goodbye to stress, you need to attack it from five angles:

- Cognitive
- Emotional
- Interpersonal
- Physical
- Spiritual

Like the five fingers of the hand, you must use all five of these stress "fingers" (Figure 4.1 on page 77). When waving goodbye to a friend, it works best to use all five fingers instead of just one (especially if that finger is the middle one). The same is true when waving goodbye to stress. The next few chapters are dedicated to your five-finger action plan to wave away stress. Each stress finger has its own chapter, so you can drill down to the basics for each and

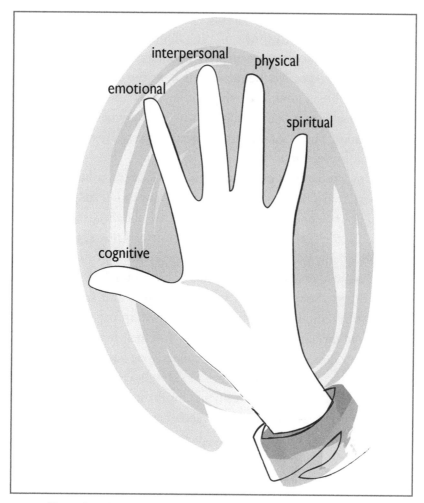

FIGURE 4.1 **illustration of the stress fingers**

spend time exploring possible solutions for less stress. To begin your journey, experiment with a solution from two fingers a day and work your way up to all five.

real solutions, real hope

Once you have studied the numerous stress solutions in the coming chapters, you'll feel better about your situation. Just knowing that you have so many options will give you a sense of freedom, hope, and choice. It's easy to forget about solutions in moments of high stress. Therefore keep these chapters bookmarked for the moments you lose this perspective. Remember, it's not the challenges at work that make or break your leadership journey. It is how you respond to those challenges that is the real secret to getting where you want to be as a leader. These solutions have been successfully tried by many executives just like you.

You're probably wondering how these stress solutions, "soft skills," or brain skills get you where you want to be. As your career ascends, your impact is less direct. Gone are the days that you can program all the code, design all the clinic's workflows, manage the total budget, approve all the website functionalities, or even handle all the customer needs and complaints yourself. Instead, you have to rely on others. Sometimes it's two contractors, and sometimes it's a team of thousands. If you are at the top of an organization, you have to lead through your direct reports and their teams as well. But regardless of how many people you manage, you have to engage with humans. And humans are, by nature, complex, smart, emotional, physiological, diverse, creative, fickle, brilliant, and beautiful, each in their own ways. Your job is to reach beyond your own stress so you can motivate, focus, and lead them to where you need them to be. Before we dive into the individual "five fingers," let's lay some groundwork. First up: You need a buddy.

get a stress support buddy

Before you start on your journey to a more joyful, effective, and stress-less life at work and at home, let's review some fundamentals.

First, on your way to a better you, you can't be a lone wolf. You need the support of at least one person to discuss your stress solution experiments with. Select this stress buddy carefully. Ideally, this is someone who will understand and support your efforts but who doesn't have a lot to gain or lose from your experiments. You want the right blend of support and objectivity. Perhaps choose a peer in a different company, your book group, your place of worship, or your gym. Or it could be somebody you run into one or two times a month, like a neighbor, a fellow student, or an acquaintance at your dog park.

You don't have to tell them your entire leadership history, the complete details of your current situation, or your career goals. Instead, just give them a copy of your experiment logs, found near the end of each of the next few chapters. Meet once or twice a month to discuss the results and observations of your experiments. This will have two positive effects. First, it will break the social isolation that surrounds stress. And second, it will help keep you on track and force you to reflect on what worked and what didn't. Don't be surprised if your stress buddy ends up trying some of your experiments on their own. Stress, after all, is very common. It might even turn into something you do as part of my stress-less groups, with a few others who can support one another to reduce and prevent stress.

small steps, big gains: experimentation

Second, let's talk about experimentation. I would like to tell you that I have a magic bullet that will eradicate all your symptoms and prevent all stress. But as you have seen, stress is caused and manifests itself in many ways. You are already ahead of the game because you know exactly where your strengths and pain points are. Now you are ready to attack them with solutions that hit the mark.

Why am I encouraging you to experiment rather than make ongoing, sustained changes? Because, just like the continuous improvement model you probably use at work, you don't yet know which solutions will work best for you. Also, there is a psychological hurdle that you are likely avoiding: You probably already feel pressed for time and overwhelmed at the thought of doing even more. This way, you can experiment with stress solutions for a day or a week. You can manage to do almost anything for that long because your brain knows there is an end, an out. Then you can refine your approach.

For example, if you try setting aside 30 minutes a day to plan your week, you might find that is too much time and that you can get away with 15 minutes. Or you might find that you can combine your planning time with your commute on the train.

chapter wrap-up

As you read the next five chapters, get ready to take action. There will be a place for you to list all the potential activities you'd like to take advantage of that address each of your five stress fingers. Choose two or three fingers to focus on at a time, and commit to them for at least two weeks. Take time to repair the current damage and prevent any further damage.

As I discuss each component of your five finger action plan to wave away stress, pay attention to what resonates with you. Take notes on the activities that apply to you now or have applied to you in the past. As you've learned, the process of healing from stress is not for the faint at heart. It requires a multipronged, rigorous, and concerted effort.

chapter 5

the cognitive finger

the first finger to wave away stress is the cognitive finger. In this chapter, I'll discuss a host of different competencies related to the cognitive effects of stress. You'll have an opportunity to select one or two activities that you can apply to your life to develop your cognitive capacity as a leader.

By now, you know that stress impairs memory and concentration. Cortisol binds to cells in the hippocampus of the brain (the area responsible for converting new experiences into memories) and disrupts the conversion process. Stress can reduce cognitive flexibility. Have you ever felt a stiffness in your joints that prevented you from moving easily? The same type of feeling happens to your brain when you're stressed.

You shouldn't take this feeling lightly. As a leader, you require top-notch cognitive skills to perform your job. Leaders in the manufacturing industry, for example, need the cognitive skills to understand the sequencing involved in supply chain procedures. Leaders in the construction industry need the cognitive visualization skills to sketch designs and blueprints. Leaders in the health-care sector need cognitive skills to understand complex diagnostic procedures.

Cognitive training (especially activities that focus on increasing concentration and memory) can improve neuroplasticity and reduce stress levels. Who ever thought a jigsaw puzzle could help you in your job? Cognitive functioning can also be improved by seeking out novelty, learning a new skill, or engaging in creative thought. Poetry, anyone?

Remember our discussion on the cognitive effects of stress from Chapter 1? Let's put your cognitive powers to the test. From memory, use the chart in Table 5.1 on page 83 to determine which of the following effects of stress are a cognitive effect.

Now it's time to focus on you. Use Table 5.2 on page 83 to assess your own cognitive health. Respond to the corresponding questions with yes ("Y") or no ("N").

tackling your cognitive stresses

Your cognitive health is often closely tied to your routine. When you stick to the same routine each day, your brain is less effective at making new pathways. New experiences stimulate new neural connections and increase neuroplasticity. For example, learning a new musical instrument requires multiple senses, so it's not surprising that it promotes brain plasticity. The association of sounds and visual patterns with motor actions can cause new neural networks to form.

Use the following table to determine whether the effects are cognitive ("Y") or not ("N").

Effect	Yes ("Y") or No ("N")
1. Loss of motivation	
2. Muscle tension	
3. Memory loss	
4. Irritability	
5. Overeating	
6. Migraines	
7. Drug or alcohol abuse	
8. Mental slowdown	

Solution: 1. "N", 2. "N", 3. "Y", 4. "N", 5." N", 6."N", 7. "N", 8. "Y"

TABLE 5.1 **quiz: cognitive effects of stress**

Question	Yes ("Y") or No ("N")
Do you ever forget family members' names?	
Do you struggle to remember driving directions?	
Do you ever forget important dates?	
Do you misplace your keys or wallet often?	

The more "Y" you responded with, the weaker your cognitive health. There is a lot of room for improvement, which should come as good news to you.

TABLE 5.2 **quiz: assess your cognitive health**

The cognitive impacts of stress can wreak havoc on your ability to lead. Let's review some of the most common cognitive effects of stress (which you read about in Chapter 1). Then, for each one, I'll give you some solutions to try out.

mental slowdown

When your mental processes slow down, it's like you're swimming through glue. It takes you longer to process new information, make decisions, and interact with colleagues. Ultimately, your stress escalates and your productivity plummets.

Are you experiencing mental slowdown? If so, your leadership capabilities are probably compromised and you are probably yearning to cope better. Let's review some of the most effective solutions at your disposal.

time to think

Leaders, and indeed all humans, have an innate bias toward action. With so few hours in the day, it's easy to try to jam as much as possible into what little time you have. But taking time to think is critical.

What to do? From this point forward, commit to adding one minute of thinking time before each of your decisions and actions. If you would normally act on impulse, allow one minute to think. If you would normally spend two minutes thinking about a decision, take three. Use this extra time to make sure you've thought through the situation. Are you overlooking any potential problems or pitfalls?

Another strategy is to allocate ten minutes a day to think about one particular topic or simply to see what comes to mind. To ensure this time to think is built into your routine, you can anchor it to an activity you never miss, such as your morning coffee or commute to work.

Example in practice: Former AOL CEO Tim Armstrong makes his employees spend 10 percent of their time just thinking.[1] This helps ensure that they don't make rash and unsound decisions before thinking through the effects.

jump-start your mind

Your brain is your source of intellectual power. There are lots of different ways to jump-start your mind. Choose one that feels natural to you.

What to do? Whenever you're tasked to complete even a semi-complex activity, make a checklist. Make the list as detailed as possible. This will prepare your brain to visualize yourself actually performing the task and will jump-start your mind out of your mental slowdown. It will also rev up your mind, maximize your time efficiency, and help ensure you don't miss anything.

When it comes to jump-starting your mind, you can also consider making a pro/con list. Any time you are tasked with making an important decision and feel your mind slowing down, draft a pro/con list. If there are several factors involved, make pro/con lists for each one. Take the time to think each side through, regardless of your gut reaction.

Visualization is another powerful way to jump-start your mind. Whenever you're experiencing mental slowdown due to nervousness about how an event will unfold, visualize it happening. Try to visualize three different versions of the event: the best outcome, the satisfactory outcome, and the nightmare outcome (recall the fear-setting exercises in Chapter 3). This type of pre-mortem activity can quell nerves. Pre-mortems can help you think about something you've overlooked. Many companies have adopted pre-mortem activities to prepare for product launches, but they can be used for any event that causes you mental slowdown based on anxiety.

Example in practice: Oprah Winfrey frequently discussed the power of visualization techniques on her talk show, likening the power of visualization to the law of attraction. That is, she believes that by engaging in visualization, you can get what you desire in life.

watch for the activity trap

Most people tend to overcommit (we'll see later in this book that women are especially prone to this in the workplace). Leaders have no shortage of tasks to attend to. It's easy to squander your time on the 98 percent of tasks that aren't really urgent. But when this happens, leaders don't leave enough time for the 2 percent of tasks that really matter. Watch out for the activity trap. It should signal multiple red flags.

What to do? Before you get started on your workday each morning, write a to-do list. It shouldn't include the 98 percent of tasks that aren't mission-critical. Only include the 2 percent, or approximately six to eight tasks, that really matter.

If your to-do lists aren't getting completed, consider drafting a to-don't list to accompany each to-do list. This can include, for example, restricting social media between 8:00 A.M. and 2:00 P.M., or eliminating that meeting you're not adding value to or you can delegate to a team member.

You may get a feeling of accomplishment from the activity trap when you check off things that don't really impact your longer-term goals, but you'll get that same feeling many times over by attending to important matters that make a big impact on your stress levels.

Example in practice: Airbnb CEO Brian Chesky has a unique approach to to-do lists. He starts each day by making a list of everything he wants to accomplish. Next he consolidates similar activities together. Finally, he asks himself whether there is one action he can take to check off all the tasks in a group.[2] This process helps him focus only on a few large endeavors each day.

turn off your "i have the answers" program

Do you feel the need to have all the answers? Perhaps your colleagues even expect you to have all the answers. If so, you might be overtaxing your mind so much that your brain's hardware is slowing down. Start to free up your mind and time by switching off your "I have the answers" program.

What to do? Tell yourself and others that no one person can have all the answers—and convince yourself that it's OK not to have them. Encourage people to research problems on their own before coming to you. It will help them become more resourceful and informed. This is a good thing.

Make sure you hire and develop experts on your team so that the company has the talent it needs to execute successfully. If you feel you have job security because you are the go-to person with all the answers, remember that everybody is replaceable. People who develop others and build strong, skilled teams are the leaders who progress in their careers.

Example in practice: Jim Whitehurst, president and CEO of Red Hat, recognizes that admitting your mistakes is a hallmark of great leadership. He sees it as a key way to become more accountable and increase engagement. Early in his career, Whitehurst chose to go to market with an acquired product that wasn't exclusively open-sourced. He decided not to rewrite the code and make it entirely open source to increase appeal. The product was met with unfavorable reviews, and Whitehurst was forced to go back to the drawing board and rewrite the code. He admitted his mistakes to the organization and gained a lot of respect in the process.

But mental slowdown is only one aspect of cognitive stress. There are many others.

difficulty concentrating

It can be hard to concentrate even on your best days. You're surrounded by distractions. When you struggle to concentrate, you can't focus on what needs to be done, waste time, and stress yourself out. It's time to review some solutions.

lay out the work and stick to it

When you embark on a task without a plan, it's like going on a road trip without a map. You need to know where you're headed. A key part of exercising your cognitive finger is to plan.

What to do? Before starting an activity, create a detailed plan of action. What do you need to do? How much time can you devote to it? Do you require any additional human support? What about other resource support? Map out your task from start to finish, and don't forget to sequence tasks and number them. This will ensure you don't overlook anything.

If you're inclined to procrastinate and can't seem to get started on your plan, try this: Tell yourself you will work on it for only ten minutes, starting in ten minutes. Even if your mind isn't tracking, start typing. The dread of starting is often greater than actually executing the task. The plan won't be perfect the first time, but that's OK. At least you've started. And once you've finalized your plan, commit to it wholeheartedly. Don't give in to interruptions!

Example in practice: Here's a cautionary example for you that showcases what can happen when you fail to plan. A few years ago, Hershey's was gung-ho about getting viral attention online and made the rash decision to change its logo from a three-dimensional Hershey's Kiss to a two-dimensional one. Had the company taken more time to plan, it might have realized that it needed to do some consumer marketing tests first. When the new logo hit, it didn't resemble a delicious chocolate treat. Instead, people complained that it looked like a piece of poo!

give away time-consuming work

You could easily spend all your waking hours on time-consuming work. Time-consuming work is like steroids for stress—the opposite of what you want. Your success depends on your ability to delegate as much time-consuming work as possible.

What to do? Embrace delegation and planning. Start each week by taking note of the people around you, their skills, and their time availability. Keep a running list. Then map out the most time-consuming work you have on your plate and align it to their skills. Make sure these employees are capable of taking on the work. If they're not, take some time to coach, train, and prepare them for the task—or, better yet, assign another manager or employee to train them.

When it comes to delegating, "I can do it faster myself," is a terrible excuse. It only results in you being overloaded and unable to concentrate. "I can do it better myself," is just as bad. It does not allow others to take on more responsibility, be recognized, or gain skills.

Establish objectives and results, and ensure commitment. If you still can't concentrate, take a look at the research on the science of delegation. Yes, there's a science to effective delegation. It involves strong communication skills and interpersonal relationships. You'll learn more when I discuss the interpersonal finger in Chapter 7. You'll also learn more about the health benefits of delegating when I review the physical finger in Chapter 8.

Example in practice: Esteemed American philanthropist Eli Broad has built KB Home and Sun America, two Fortune 500 companies. Broad credits much of his success to being able to delegate. He sees the inability to delegate as one of the biggest leadership problems. He advises leaders to focus on the most important tasks and find a way to delegate anything else.

pay attention to where your mind wanders

Everyone's mind wanders. It's natural. Sometimes your mind goes to happy places, sometimes to sad places, and sometimes to fearful places. But unless you're in a highly creative field, mind wandering can disrupt productivity. It's in your best interest to pay close attention to where your mind is venturing.

What to do? The next time you find your mind wandering, go with it and take a moment to reflect. Where is your mind headed? Is it a passion area? Is it an underlying worry? If the latter, jot down a quick note and schedule some time in your calendar to think about it later. If you're preparing for a big presentation at work and your mind keeps drifting to worrying that you've forgotten to lock your front door, it can derail your focus. Take action. Phone a neighbor or make a quick trip home. When you return, you'll be better able to focus on the task at hand.

If your mind is wandering to a vacation, another job, another career, or another life, then make time to think about why this might be happening in more detail. Consider talking to an expert about it.

Example in practice: One of my clients is a former VP at a furniture sales business. He approached me with concerns that his mind often wandered to thinking about store design. He always looked forward to the holiday season. He loved to visit the stores and see their holiday setup designs and decorations. This was clearly a passion area, so we finally decided to take action. The VP enrolled in a three-month interior design class, which ultimately led him to clinch a promotion in operations and then a promotion to the COO position. Pay attention to where your mind wanders. It's likely trying to tell you something.

do nothing

Everyone needs downtime. It's important to stop and take a break occasionally. If you're constantly in ready-aim-fire mode, your fight-or-flight response is always switched on, and your cortisol levels will be sky-high. Sometimes the only way to get your cortisol back down to healthy levels is to stop. Doing nothing can be a recipe for success.

What to do? Carve out 10 to 15 minutes. Find a quiet space, close the door, turn off all your devices, and close your eyes if you want to. Focus on your breath as you inhale and exhale. Remove yourself from all sources of stress. Let all your worries, fears, and apprehensions float away. After 15 minutes, you'll find you're able to concentrate more effectively. That brief reprieve can be just what you need to regain a state of balance.

Example in practice: Whenever I have a full-day on-site visit scheduled with a client, I proactively build in 15 minutes to do nothing. I know these on-sites are all-consuming. During those 15 minutes, I devote myself completely to inaction. I find a comfortable place, turn off all devices, and sit down. I close my eyes, focus on my breathing, and listen as the oxygen flows through my lungs. When I resume my work, I feel like a different person: rejuvenated and ready to tackle whatever comes next. There's a hidden value in empty time.

Concentration difficulties often go hand in hand with several other cognitive effects of stress. One of the most common is feeling overwhelmed.

feeling overwhelmed

When you feel overwhelmed, you may feel a sense of fog come over you. You feel paralyzed, you have difficulty thinking clearly, and you can react rashly to situations. It becomes hard for you to see a way out or a way through your problems. But there are many stress solutions you can experiment with.

be clear about annual goals and objectives

Leaders often get distracted by fire drills at work: Urgent problems that are irrelevant to the current business plan and an endless stream of daily distractions, such as emails that could be assigned to others, occupy their time. Do not fall victim to these traps.

What to do? Write your personal, departmental, or company-wide top three or five annual goals on Post-it notes. Place them on your wall at work, on your laptop, in your pocket, on your fridge, and everywhere else you can think of. The more visible, the better. Then prioritize your time so that you can accomplish them. Anything else (within reason) does not deserve your attention. Simply ask yourself: "Does this matter help us meet this year's goals?" If the answer is yes, then take care of it. If the answer is no, then let it be.

Example in practice: Intel has perfected the art of annual planning. Its approach is both top-down and bottom-up. In theory, each division creates its own plans, which then combine as part of a larger group plan. The process is time-consuming, underscoring its importance. It typically begins in September and may continue into January.[3]

get help from others

When you get stuck in a thought loop or lost in your blank mind, it's easy to get overwhelmed. To get unstuck, reach out to other people. Don't think you need to be a lone wolf. You will find others will want to help you, and you'll feel more connected to them. And when you hear yourself describe the business or personal situation out loud, you'll immediately gain a new perspective on the problem.

What to do? Find a friend, coworker, or family member to talk to. Pick up the phone. Better yet, meet them in person. The people you talk to are bound to have great ideas, which will help your thought processes come back to life. You don't have to (and probably can't) use all their ideas. But listening to them will help you anyway. There will be a jewel or two for you to use. Remember that old saying about how two heads are better than one? If you have reservations about accepting help from others, take a look at Chapter 6, which describes solutions for the emotional aspects of stress, such as trust and building teams.

Example in practice: Consider tech exec Marissa Mayer, who frequently sought advice from Google cofounders Larry Page and Sergey Brin. (Mayer was Google's 20th hire and their first female engineer.) Even after she became CEO of rival search engine Yahoo!, she turned to Page and Brin when she faced challenges navigating the organizational hierarchy and the tech industry. She credits a lot of her success to their support.

define the problem

Sometimes leaders forget to define the very problem that is vexing them. Sometimes it's a problem they have already set up systems to address, but when they are overwhelmed, they confuse the problems with symptoms or even solutions. This can happen with problems involving people, technology, or the core of the business itself.

What to do? All effective problem solving starts with a definition. It can be tempting to rely on past experiences, biases, and premature conclusions when defining the problem. But this will hamper your ability to identify the problem. The best method is to stop and peel the onion. Start to write out the problem, or what seems to be the problem, until you can get to its very core. Break the problem down into its smallest pieces. Ask a lot of questions, especially "Why?"

Example in practice: Whenever I perform client work, I review the assessment I've done for them and remind myself of the exact problem the organization is facing. With my many years of experience, it's easy for me to jump to conclusions. It's always important that the client and I take a step back and define the problem throughout our projects.

take a more strategic approach

As a leader, sometimes stress can overwhelm your cognitive abilities. You might forget to act strategically and move the business forward. You might be limited to working at a unit manager level rather than at an executive level. You need to lead at the highest level your skills allow, be informed about your business, track or set current market trends, and always have a view to the future of your organization.

What to do? Spend time with your customers. Don't ask them what your current products or services are doing for them. Instead, ask what they would like them to do. Imagine, dream, and tap into possibilities together. Engage in open-ended conversations. And listen. You might gain some valuable knowledge about your competitors or potential business partners.

Another stress solution you can use to tackle strategy is to get out into the world. It's simple, but it's underleveraged by companies. The best products were designed by people who listened to the fantastical. Get out, meet people, travel, watch new shows and plays, and watch people. Play "What If?" What if more of the population were older than 70? What would they need? Would they have more buying power? How would your international strategy change if the U.S. dollar were cheaper in China than in Vietnam? What if the three companies who own all your consumer data merged?

Strategic thinking can be a double-edged sword. It can easily make you feel more overwhelmed, rather than less. This is because it involves building on assumptions that can change and reading into the future. But take the risk. Just avoid sharing your strategies right away, or share them only with a couple of people you trust. The main goal is to loosen up your thinking.

Strategic thinking builds on itself. You need outside inputs to inform, stimulate, and galvanize your process. So read business magazines, watch interviews of leaders online, and attend conferences and meetings that are strategic rather than operational in nature (or, better yet, outside your field).

Example in practice: Kodak, like many companies, experienced overwhelming stress that precluded strategy. Kodak massively contributed to the digital age by inventing the first digital camera in the 1970s, but it bet heavily on its rapidly growing film business instead. This overemphasis meant that Kodak's leaders couldn't keep track of customers' need for easier camera technologies. The company then chose to double down on marketing its established products, even as the digital camera market was exploding and it was earning billions from its patent. Kodak ultimately filed for bankruptcy in 2012.

be creative

Feeling overwhelmed limits your ability to be creative, but being creative is key to overcoming that feeling and improving as a leader.

What to do? Remove any roadblocks that are preventing you from being creative. Perhaps you're a perfectionist. Perhaps you don't have enough time. Perhaps you're worried about how others will perceive you. Carve out some dedicated time to be creative. This will give you a space to exercise your creative juices. Let your mind wander. Ask broad questions. Switch concepts and jump freely from one idea to another. This can transition your thinking from your left-hemisphere brain functions to your right.

Another stress solution for creativity involves some standard problem-solving skills. I recommend drawing out your problem on a storyboard. Place all the characters on the storyboard: colleagues, customers, systems, processes, or departments. Throw it all out there.

Creativity involves freedom of thought first and design structure later. Don't jump straight to the latter. For example, in this book, I encourage you to experiment with one or two solutions related to each of your five stress fingers within a defined period of time. This is, in many ways, a creative process. You're trying a bunch of techniques to see what works before settling on your final stress-reduction program.

Example in practice: Each day, I take ten minutes to walk outside and just let my mind wander. I ask a lot of questions about the world around me, which helps reframe my state of mind and my thinking processes. I find this helps me be more creative. The buzzing traffic, people, dogs, trees, architecture from different eras, and overheard conversations stimulate my creative juices and cause me to spot connections I wouldn't otherwise have seen.

When you're overwhelmed, among the many other issues it can cause is the significant impact it can have on your memory. Memory loss or impairment is another common cognitive stress effect.

memory loss or impairment

Stress often results in forgetfulness or confusion. You may find yourself forgetting a colleague's name or failing to follow up on an important email. This can cause a lot of frustration. Chronic stress can cause permanent damage to memory functioning. Let's look at what you can do about it.

count to ten

It happens to everyone. You lose track of your thoughts midstream, sometimes in front of other people. Try not to draw attention to yourself. Just continue on to another thought and try to keep your composure. Embarrassment will only stress you and your memory more.

What to do? Count to ten in your head. This will help you keep your composure. Ironically, your memory often returns once your mind is thinking about something else. For example, as you struggle to remember which building the finance department is in now, move on to your next point, or even ponder what you and your team will be having for lunch. Changing your focus seems to prompt memory.

Example in practice: My neighbor recently told me that whenever he walks into his living room and forgets what he came there for, he goes into the kitchen and does something else. He ends up remembering what he wanted more quickly than if he stood in the middle of the living room racking his brain. It's like magic.

schedule tasks in your calendar

There's a lot going on in your mind. You can only hold so many details in your short-term memory, even at the best of times. Stress impedes short-term memory due to the hormones it releases into your bloodstream. A calendar is an effective way to jog your memory, keep track of your time and tasks, and prevent memory loss or impairment.

What to do? Use your calendar without fail. Block off enough time to do all the tasks you hope to accomplish each day. List all your tasks. Make sure to include time for breaks and travel. By scheduling tasks into your calendar, you'll ensure they don't become clouded in your mind.

You should also share your calendar with a trusted party, especially a co-worker. Too many leaders have assistants or project managers that are underused and with whom they don't even share their calendars.

As the brain ages, short-term memory fades. Leaders with years of valuable experience and expertise can waste their short-term memory by getting bogged down with time and task management.

Example in practice: In addition to being a proponent of to-do lists, Richard Branson schedules tasks in his calendar. This helps him avoid forgetting about all the meetings, activities, and other tasks he gets done in a day. Branson has even recommended that we schedule time to dream on our calendars! Give it a try.

consult a time/task management expert

People are quick to ask an expert when they have questions about technical concepts, whether it's product design or fixing a bike. Why aren't they as quick to ask for help with productivity and stress? Beats me.

Your memory can be improved with enhanced time management skills. A time management expert can help.

What to do? Find someone you know who always seems to get tasks done on time and that you know is good at time management. Reach out to them and ask them to coach you for an hour. Be a sponge. Absorb their tips, advice, and words of wisdom. Soak in as much as you can.

Example in practice: Early in my career, I coached a new manager who struggled with time management. Her to-do lists didn't seem to work for her. I owe a lot of my great time management techniques to my mom, who was a teacher and was terrific at time management. Throughout my early life, she shared many tips with me, including reducing distractions and creating "to-don't" lists, both of which I shared with my client. She has been more effective at time management ever since. If you're wondering, my to-don't list included no technology, people, or snacks while I was writing this book.

memory exercises

Your brain can quickly atrophy when it is underused, putting a damper on your memory. Your memory is valuable—you need to protect it. A great way to do this is to perform memory exercises. I'm a particular fan of memory recall exercises.

What to do? Choose a memory exercise to perform at least three times a week. Crossword puzzles, jigsaw puzzles, sudoku puzzles, memory recall exercises, optical illusions, and brain teasers are all great.

Example in practice: I use the many lists I create each week to play memory recall games. Any time I finish making a list, I take a minute before spending as much time as I need to memorize the list. Next I set the timer on my phone for one hour and continue my day. When the timer buzzes, I try to recall the list from memory.

When I first started the exercise, I was awful. Five-item lists were my limit. But as I practiced, I improved. Last week, I remembered a 16-item grocery list. What number of items might you be willing to experiment with?

your cognitive stress experiments

You've just learned a boatload of strategies to deal with the cognitive impacts of stress. Your mind is likely working overtime thinking of ways to improve how you think and your cognitive capabilities as a leader and human. Now let's keep track of it all.

Using Table 5.3 on page 98, list your current cognitive problems. You can select from a problem we've discussed or choose something else. In the second column of the table, list any cognitive improvement activities you currently perform on a regular basis. Don't worry if you don't do any. That just means there's more room for improvement. Now list one or two new cognitive stress solutions you are committing to do, starting tomorrow. Choose from any of the stress solutions described above.

I recommend moderation. You don't want to overwhelm yourself, commit to too much, and end up doing nothing. Instead, pick one or two solutions and try your hand (or head) at them for a limited time. These are your experiments, so you should decide when you will start and when you will stop each one. Write this in the fourth column. It's always easier to commit to doing a new activity for one day or one week than forever. And remember to enlist a friend for support and accountability!

Here are step-by-step instructions for how to complete the stress solution worksheet in Table 5.3:

▶ *Cognitive problem.* Describe the issue you are trying to solve.
▶ *What I'm doing now.* List how you've been trying to solve it.

1. Cognitive Problem	2. What I'm Doing Now	3. Experimental Stress Solution	4. Start and End Date	5. Results and Observations

TABLE 5.3 **cognitive stress experiment log**

▹ *Experimental stress solution.* Explain what new stress solution(s) you will experiment with.

▹ *Start and end date.* List start and end dates of the new stress solution(s).

▹ *Results and observations.* Write out the results of the experiment. Describe what you observed, what you learned, and any adjustments you might make in the future. Will you continue with this stress solution or try something else?

chapter wrap-up

Do you find yourself forgetting why you walked into a room? Forgetting names and facts that used to be at the tip of your tongue? Are you distracted at work, or even at home, for no good reason? Don't worry. By selecting one or two stress solutions to experiment with, you're well on your way to improving your cognitive functioning.

It's now time to move on to your second stress finger: the emotional finger.

the emotional finger

Y ou learned about the emotional effects of stress in Chapter 1. The strength of your emotional finger largely depends on your level of self-awareness. Self-awareness is your ability to recognize and understand your emotions. Without this ability, you can't determine how your emotions affect you and the people around you.

When you exercise your emotional finger, it's a powerful thing. No matter how optimistic or pessimistic you are, you can rewire your thinking. You can look at the glass as either half-empty or half-full. When you change your mind, you can also change your emotions and learn to see things from others' perspectives. In doing so, you will gain compassion, improve your problem-solving skills, and ultimately make better decisions. Take the quiz in Figure 6.1 below to see how self-aware you are.

Respond to the following statements with yes ("Y") or no ("N").

Statement	Yes ("Y") or No ("N")
It's difficult for me to recognize my emotions.	
People say I act before I think.	
I have a poor understanding of my strengths and weaknesses.	
When I'm mad, the people around me know it.	
When I'm mad or frustrated, I don't know how to calm myself down.	

The more "N" you responded with, the more self-aware you're likely to be.

FIGURE 6.1 **quiz: how self-aware are you?**

Your level of self-awareness is closely related to the emotional effects of stress. When you're stressed, your level of self-awareness declines. Recall the discussion of the emotional effects of stress from Chapter 1. Let's put your emotional muscles to the test. Determine which of the following effects of stress is an emotional effect in Figure 6.2 on page 103.

Emotional training is something that most people don't think enough about. It includes learning compassion, gratitude, emotional management, and emotional intelligence. Like cognitive training, emotional training is another stress minimizer. It's the second finger

Effect	Yes ("Y") or No ("N")
1. Loss of motivation	
2. Muscle tension	
3. Memory loss	
4. Irritability	
5. Overeating	
6. Migraines	
7. Drug or alcohol abuse	
8. Mental slowdown	

Solution: 1."Y", 2."N", 3."N", 4."Y", 5."N", 6."N", 7."N", 8."N"

Solution: 1 and 4

FIGURE 6.2 **quiz: emotional effects of stress**

needed to wave goodbye to stress. Emotional intelligence (EQ or EI), which is defined as your ability to recognize and regulate your own and others' emotions, has been found to be an especially strong predictor of stress. Research has found that acquiring EQ skills can significantly reduce psychological stress among adolescents.[1]

In fact, EQ is one of the most powerful predictors of professional success. A high EQ enables you to handle pressure well, understand and cooperate with others, give and receive feedback constructively, and engage in more effective decision making. As an executive, a high EQ enables you to stand out from the masses. A 2011 survey by CareerBuilder found that 75 percent of managers and HR professionals are more likely to promote an employee with a high EQ and (comparatively speaking) lower IQ than an individual with a high IQ and lower EQ.[2] EQ is becoming more and more top-of-mind for companies in their recruiting efforts. Check your EQ in the quiz in Figure 6.3 on page 104.

Respond to the following statements according to whether they are true ("T") or false ("F").

Statement	True ("T") or False ("F")
When I'm criticized, I don't tend to become defensive.	
I'm usually able to see things from another person's perspective.	
I tend to voice my concerns calmly and with poise.	
I tend to think before I act.	
I'm generally able to stay calm in times of high stress. I can stay calm under pressure.	

The more "T"s you responded with, the higher your EQ level is likely to be.

FIGURE 6.3 **quiz: do you have a high eq?**

Don't be discouraged if your EQ isn't as high as you'd like it to be. You can improve your EQ, but it requires a dedicated effort. Pay attention to how you behave, especially in stressful situations. Question your own opinions. Does your co-worker have a valid point? Predict and visualize how you will feel in certain situations. What if your boss curtly rejects a proposal that you've toiled away at for months? Funnel your emotions into something productive and positive.

Many of the highest-performing leaders keep a diary to help enhance their EQ skills. Far too often, people are too quick to dismiss their feelings and don't take the time to think about their meaning and significance. Keeping a diary can help you detect patterns and encourage you to reflect on how your emotional states are influenced by your experiences. Only after you take the time to look inward can you shift your focus outward.

In this chapter, you will read about how you as a leader can develop your emotional finger to wave away stress and use your EQ skills to both solve and prevent the emotional impacts of stress. As in Chapter 5, we'll walk through some of the most common signs of stress and discuss steps you can take to minimize its effects.

irritability

When you feel irritable, you feel agitated and become upset easily. You're likely to lash out at others. This is never good. But when your colleagues may perceive it as intimidation, it's even worse. Let's review some tools available to you.

count to ten

When people are emotional, they tend to make rash and impulsive decisions. More often than not, these decisions are not the best ones. They're often far from it. It's important to learn to slow down, especially when you're emotional.

What to do? Whenever you feel that you might lose your composure, count to ten before reacting or take a few seconds (or even minutes) to do something else. Don't panic. This will make things worse, especially if you're in public. People take their cues from you. You don't want to lose their respect, or worse yet, set a cultural tone of irritability. Choose something mindless to do during those ten seconds. If you're on the phone, take a walk around your desk. Read a news headline. Do anything to regain your composure. If you need to, count to 60 seconds or close your eyes and count 60 sheep.

Another stress solution for irritability is acting as if you are calm even if you aren't. Pay attention to your body language. Relax your shoulders and smile.

Example in practice: When I am irritated with traffic while driving, I turn on my favorite tune or podcast. I often feel there are never enough hours in a day to listen to them, so why not take advantage of the delay to do something I enjoy? And when I am annoyed because I can't seem to write the way I want to, I give myself ten minutes to look at cute animal videos. It works like a charm. Life is too short to spend it needlessly irritated, and nobody feels inspired by a grouch.

find your triggers

Often, but especially when you are stressed, your irritability is caused by a specific trigger or triggers. Your fuse is shorter when you are stressed. If other leaders are stressed, too, remember that their fuses might be shorter as well. Have you ever noticed that some projects have a distinct aura of irritation? This tends to happen because the same people are stressed, and they are repeatedly being triggered or triggering each other at the same time. It's important to play detective and find these triggers. After all, to know yourself is to empower yourself as a leader and as a human.

What to do? As soon as you find yourself reacting to something that irritates you, try to trace the feeling back to its cause and make a note of it. Do this periodically throughout the day. Do any themes emerge?

As a longer-term stress solution, consider using a journal to record your feelings. You can even do this on your phone or via emails to yourself. When you have 10 to 15 minutes, stop and reflect; you'll likely be able to pinpoint the underlying issue. Is it one employee at work who can't seem to master something? Perhaps your impatience with him reflects your need for perfection or reminds you that you didn't take the time to make sure he had the right training.

Look further back in time and determine if the triggers remind you of somebody. Perhaps your first boss was tough on you, and you've inadvertently taken on some of her characteristics, such as showing irritability at work. If there is a persistent trigger, you're bound to be triggered again in the future. Develop a plan for how you will respond. Good leaders act and look like leaders at all times.

Example in practice: Nelson Mandela was diligent about keeping a diary, which helped him to record his thoughts and reflect on his experiences. The process was enormously enlightening and helped him persevere on his quest for freedom.

downsize the conflict

Conflicts can quickly morph into status battles, particularly if there have been chronic stressors with colleagues. It's important to take time to downsize the conflict.

What to do? After a conflict has started to brew, look for points of agreement and jot them down on a notepad. Next, write down the open items. Focus on common objectives and priorities, try to keep the discussion concrete, and don't worry about abstract concepts or judgments. Instead, concentrate on facts and specific details. This will help you decide on a more actionable game plan. If certain points of contention are inconsequential, don't let them bog you down. Onward and upward!

Above all, focus on the most important issues. If you need to, collect more evidence or do more research. Whenever my clients are engaged in a conflict, I ask them to write down all points of agreement first.

Example in practice: One of my clients reached out to me when one of her departments was getting ready to move buildings. The leaders engaged a wonderful mover with the patience of a saint. Still, a couple of the leaders were lobbying for treasured cubicles for their teams. Sure, wanting the best for your team is honorable. But in this case, it was being done at the expense of others.

The mover ultimately asked the two leaders to meet with her. She skillfully opened by asking if the leaders wanted the sharing of real estate to be fair and collaborative. They both said yes, and the three of them were able to come up with a floor plan that was fair to all. The mover had downsized the conflict between them, without my help! Ever since, she and I have partnered on projects. She does the moving, and I do the change management. She has a superb leadership style, and her team of movers has been with her for decades.

invest less at work

You spend most of your waking days in the workplace, so it's easy to get overly invested in work. This can quickly cause leaders to become irritable, especially when things are not perfect. Sometimes they start to resent the time and energy they pour into work. They become too eager to earn raises and promotions and grow impatient with the people around them. Put work in its rightful place, for you and for your team.

What to do? Reassess the importance of work in your overall life. Ensure that your self-esteem, self-worth, mood, sense of belonging, identity, and the bulk of your social life are not dependent on your work. Sure, work is important. But make sure it holds the right place for you. Entrepreneurs and solopreneurs can be especially vulnerable to overinvesting in work. Does work hold the importance you want it to? Make sure you have a balance that suits you. And remember, its importance can change with the phases of your life.

A second stress solution involves finding a hobby. It can be a physical activity like swimming or biking, or it can be an artistic endeavor like poetry or painting. Whatever your chosen hobby, it must be an outlet for release. By releasing your built-up steam and pressure into the hobby, you'll avoid spewing it in the workplace. When you make a conscious effort to remove yourself from work, you gain perspective and realize there might be other important things or people in life.

Example in practice: Netflix CEO Reed Hastings is adamant about setting a healthy work-life balance. He makes a practice of taking six weeks of vacation every year. The time off helps him come back to the office rejuvenated and in a better state of mind. It also helps set a positive example for employees, encouraging them to engage in healthy work-life practices too.

stop causing unnecessary conflict

When you're irritable and stressed, your body language and words can get the best of you and cause unnecessary conflict. As a leader, people take their cues from you about how they should behave. Some employees are comfortable with conflict, but most are not. Since you're already stressed, it's important to be proactive about avoiding unnecessary conflict.

What to do? Pay attention to your tone of voice. Is it sharp? Cold? Are you apt to retort quickly or raise your voice? Do you tend to use a negative tone? Do you use abrupt language? Or are you likely to aim for well-thought-out solutions and act as a calm and trusted authority figure? Be sure to use an approachable and warm tone and throw in a relaxed smile. Use neutral and inclusive language. Avoid using "you and me" or "us and them." Instead, describe the situation. Take the time to ask questions before proposing solutions, and include others so you can clearly assess the issue. You should include them again in the thought process and decision-making stages. Celebrate diverse and creative viewpoints. When you aim for inclusivity, you'll gain self-awareness and will be more likely to avoid unnecessary conflict.

Also consider whether, given your level of seniority, you need to be included in the conversation at all. Could somebody else handle the situation better? I see many stressed senior leaders getting involved in conversations that should be handled by people two or three levels below them, which can cause them to get into conflicts they might or might not be able to handle effectively.

Example in practice: I had a client who appeared as if he was picking a fight each year at the final budget review meeting. He was bored with the process, and it showed. It wasn't until I suggested that one of his managers might benefit from taking the lead in the final review meetings that he decided he could let go. My client was relieved to not have to attend, and his direct report enjoyed the developmental opportunity. The whole tone of that meeting changed from combative to positive.

handle feelings gone awry

When leaders are irritable and stressed, they often lash out. Some leaders have such strong feelings that they express those feelings in ways they regret. Sometimes leaders publicly demonstrate other emotions, like tearing up or getting confused. Other leaders experience temporary alexithymia, which happens when they are unsure of what they are feeling. Does any of that sound familiar?

What to do? Try to stop it before it starts. As soon as you feel any strong emotion starting, take a quick bathroom break and do something completely different. Call somebody you love, look at football scores, or thumb through pictures of your pets. This will help you cool off and distance yourself so you can choose how to respond instead of reacting in the heat of the moment.

Also remember that this is not personal. Even if the other person takes it that way, make sure you don't. Don't get triggered, hooked, or myopic. Instead, transition to a neutral stance in your mind, as if you're solving a puzzle. Use language like "the situation" or "the event" rather than "you" or "me." It's easier to brainstorm solutions together this way.

Another solution is to try smiling or cracking a joke to defuse your body language and change how you are coming across. This might change the other person's emotions as well, resetting the tone of the interaction and allowing more positive emotions to brew.

Example in practice: A client of mine, the CEO of a medium-sized tech company, once laid off 3,000 employees over two years and still managed to soldier on and act as everybody's tower of strength. One morning, he teared up while he was giving his monthly welcome to new employees. It was inspiring to everybody in the room, as if he was a saint. In reality, he was feeling guilt and sorrow toward those he had laid off and hoped he would never need to lay off these enthusiastic new employees in front of him. He finished his welcome, went to his office, and called me immediately.

While irritability is a stress response that causes you to lash out at others, anxiety, another common emotional effect of stress, turns that response inward on you.

anxiety

Stress and anxiety go hand in hand. Anxiety is a feeling of worry, fear, or uneasiness. You often worry about uncertain events in the future. When anxiety is prolonged, it can take a heavy toll on your body, leading to enormous distress and causing clouded thinking and impulsive reactions. But there's a lot you can do to reduce it.

take and lead change in increments

When you have your eye fixed on a distant finish line, you're likely to become overburdened by all the work you must do. Instead, take and lead change in increments, one step at a time.

What to do: Don't begin a task with a poorly defined problem. Instead, make sure you know exactly what problem you're trying to solve. Look for precedents you can follow because the chances are high that somebody somewhere has tried to do this before. Make one decision at a time, and evaluate its effect before moving on.

Then take it one step further by getting feedback so you can reevaluate each step before making the next decision. Remember that it's not a race to the finish line. Races only add stress. The goal is to take and lead change in increments to prevent unnecessary anxiety. The more uncertain you are about the path to the end, the more mistakes you'll make and the more you'll veer off-course. It's best to break things down into small pieces, both for success and for anxiety control.

Example in practice: Game producer Zynga is one of many companies that failed to take and lead change in increments. It was so hungry for growth that it began spending haphazardly and without careful thought. It depended heavily on Facebook and didn't appreciate that overreliance. Had the company slowed down and taken its time to grow as an entirely separate entity with minimal dependence on Facebook, it would likely have been more successful.

let go of control and the past

When leaders are anxious, they sometimes cling to what they know, whether it's situations, lines of business, markets, or people. They try to control things and do business "the way we've always done it." In order to change, you must let go of the illusions of control and of the past.

What to do? Reflect on your current situation. Now visualize a different and more effective outcome. Then another, and another.

The exercise will start to pry you loose from your stranglehold on the past and defuse the impending sense of doom you associate with change. Try batting around your more exciting thoughts with a colleague.

Another stress solution: Go back in time about ten years. What products or services were hot in your company or your industry, and which companies paved the way? Can you even remember them? Probably not too well. That's how fast people forget things that seemed so very important at the time. Your current situation will fade in much the same way. "The way we've always done it" would have left you using your pager or flip phone.

It can be brutally difficult to let go of colleagues, business partners, or vendors. These are important relationships for all kinds of reasons. They increase your sense of belonging and teamwork. You appreciate that they've helped or mentored you. Maybe you just associate them with a meaningful time in your life. But people move on and relationships change. You can keep the good memories while adapting and leading in the present and future.

Example in practice: Years ago, I received a call from an old client who wanted change management help to abandon one kind of phone and adopt another. At first I couldn't believe it. Admittedly, the move was between two very different types of phones, but really? People at the company couldn't imagine making this transition in one day. IT was distributing manuals, which, although well-intentioned, made the situation worse. Finally, I suggested that I be filmed as I picked up and used the new phone for the first time myself. As I did, I was confused, frustrated, and even a little embarrassed, but I muddled through it. It felt like hours, but in reality, it took me just 30 minutes to understand basic controls on the new phone. I let go of control, and people found it funny and endearing. They saw the humanity and the feasibility of it all. And everybody made the transition just fine.

find humor

When used properly, humor can be a wonderfully effective antidote against anxiety and stress. At a physiological level, your own "happy substances" are released, such as dopamine and endorphins, which ward off your stress hormones. Take time to find humor, both in yourself and in others.

What to do? Not everyone is meant for stand-up comedy, but everyone can find humor in their lives. Think about your hobbies, vacations, and recent situations you found yourself in. Did something unexpected happen on your daily commute? Humor helps create a more trusting environment.

In addition, self-humor tends to be seen as positive and often results in increased respect. Isn't it interesting that by being the topic of a joke, people gain respect from others? When you let yourself be vulnerable, you humanize yourself and establish a connection to others.

Example in practice: I forgot to take off my night guard before going to work last week. Imagine my surprise when I started talking (more like mumbling) to my neighbor on the train! It was embarrassing, but it made for a great Monday morning story.

don't expect to succeed the first time

Life would be great if you got everything right the first time around. But would it be as fulfilling, and would you learn as much? If you focus only on getting things right the first time, you'll only come up with stale and safe solutions. A key way to overcome anxiety is to give yourself the freedom to get things wrong.

What to do? Give yourself more time in the batting cage, and you'll increase your opportunities to learn. Many of my clients have anxiety about public speaking. If you currently practice public speaking once each week, consider upping your commitment to three times per week. Get feedback from the audience or video footage whenever possible, and don't be scared to enlist the help of experts. Above all, expect to fail the first few times. And feel proud—it's harder to learn when you're embarrassed. Leaders preach continuous learning, but they sometimes forget to apply it to themselves.

Example in practice: Consider this book. It is based on maximizing stress-less leadership by doing experiments. You're asked to apply stress solutions for limited periods of time. The concept of experimentation helps remove the anxiety. You probably won't get all the solutions right the first time, and the ones you do get right probably won't work forever. Life is about learning. Leadership is even more about continuous learning because there are so many variables at play and things to learn about, including changing industries and leading people.

build or assign a task force

Complex problems require complex thinking, and you can feel anxious when you can't solve problems with your usual means. Relax—there's a different business solution. The next time you're slated to take on a complex initiative, consider building a task force.

What to do? There's strength in expertise. People feel more confident when they're supported by sharp minds. A key way to reduce anxiety is to build or assign a task force. Aim to recruit individuals from different areas of expertise, businesses, or industries. Teams of professionals with diverse skills and backgrounds are more likely to come up with creative and innovative solutions.

Example in practice: When one of my clients started to post profits, the CEO and the vice president of HR wanted to reward the employees and contractors who had stayed loyal through the tough times. They had thought of two possible options: a public recognition event in which three people would be anointed as Champions and cash bonuses per level of seniority. I told them I would be hard-pressed to think of something worse if I tried. Just because you are a compensation expert does not mean you understand how to reward people.

I urged them to engage a small team of trusted colleagues across different areas of the company, clarify the goal, and present the maximum budget and the timeline. The team discussed many options, including spa days, on-site massage, lunch with the CEO, a letter from the CEO, extra days off, a volunteer day, company bowling day, and beer on Fridays. They unanimously settled on one thing: cash after tax, the same amount for all employees. They reasoned that life is expensive in their city and everybody could choose what to do with their money. Employee roles had changed so much as the company had grown that they felt differentiating by title or seniority didn't take into account the extra work people had put in. And they expressly did not want a public recognition of individuals as they felt this might have negative interpersonal consequences. When the checks went out, people felt rewarded and appreciated—and understood.

At its worst, anxiety can feel paralyzing. Lack of motivation, an especially common stress symptom, can have an equally bad effect on your ability to get things done.

lack of motivation

When you lack motivation, the simplest things can feel challenging. You become disengaged and unfocused and fall into a state of paralysis that hurts your career. Since organizations rely on leaders who motivate and engage the work force, this is not just a personal problem. It's also an organizational issue that can drive down employee performance and retention. But there are many ways to prevent stress from sapping your motivation.

get a partner

Sometimes it's hard to be a lone ranger. It's easier when you have support. When you find yourself losing motivation or are fearful that you might, consider enlisting a partner.

What to do? The next time you're trying to reengage in a project at work, discuss your deliverables with a colleague. Merely talking about it might reignite your interest. And the fact that your co-worker is tracking your deliverables will help you stay accountable.

When learning a new field, competency, or market, find someone who needs to master the same area. Share observations and data, give each other advice and feedback, and encourage each other toward your goals. As you've already learned, the benefits of social support can be enormous in all aspects of your life. I've observed that the best leaders attend all kinds of seminars, presentations, and events. The very best attend events that might seem unrelated to their industry.

Example in practice: A previous client of mine had been the director of marketing for a small legal firm and tried to reengage me because she wanted to become a marketing consultant, providing social media services for small firms in the same industry. I told her, "You don't need an executive coach; you need a buddy." So we found a local meet-up where other social media consultants gathered; she met a great buddy there, and they helped each other tremendously. I also told her about the Small Business Administration (SBA), which offers reasonably priced courses on the technical elements of social media. Today, she is happy as a clam in her new profession, and so are her clients. In fact, she occasionally designs my illustrations.

track your progress

It's easy to lose sight of how far you've come, particularly when you are stressed. Sometimes leaders need to remind themselves of their progress so they can continue being engaged and motivated leaders. Many leaders and organizations make a point of tracking their progress, either on a quarterly or annual basis.

What to do? To keep your motivation to lead at peak levels, track your progress. Set goals, key performance indicators, and benchmarks. Keep a record of your team's and your own progress. Build in rewards for your team and yourself. When you reach important milestones, reward everyone with a bonus or seats at a conference. Keeping track of your progress will motivate everyone. And remember to let your boss or board of directors know about your accomplishments!

Example in practice: German online fashion retailer Zalando is one of the many companies that have adopted the objectives and key results (OKR) system. The OKR system measures and quantifies work, ensuring each employee has a concrete understanding of what everyone else is working on and how they are tracking toward their goals. Zalando grades OKR performance on a score from zero to one. To motivate employees to set a few stretch goals, 0.7 is considered the "sweet spot."[3]

say no

Leaders are naturally inclined to say "yes," which can quickly make them overloaded, overworked, and unmotivated to face the really important work. Your time is precious, especially when you're already stressed. So take a step back and say "no" when you need to. This will give you more time and energy for the work that actually does have to be done right this second.

What to do? Whenever you're asked to do something, take a moment before you respond. Ask yourself whether you have the time, skill set, and resources to do it. If not, learn how to say "no." The first step is realizing that saying "no" isn't selfish. It really means you are living up to your existing, more strategic commitments. Learn to remove the guilt from your decision-making process.

When saying "no," try the following approach: "I appreciate your request. Thank you for bringing it to me directly. Since your idea has merit, and since it comes from you, I've given this a lot of thought. As a leader who likes to say 'yes,' I would like to take everything on. But I have learned that I have to prioritize my efforts in order to be effective for the company. I'm sorry that I have to say 'no' because I have already committed to x and y."

Another stress solution involves delaying the discussion, decision, or work. Say you will consider it at a later point, either at the end of the fiscal year, when your current top-of-mind project is finished, or when you have more hands to put on the team.

It can also be effective to accept the request conditionally. Think about how to alter it so that it would be acceptable to you. For example, say, "If you assign a project manager from your team who can ensure the project stays on time and budget, then I will look into testing the product."

Example in practice: Fast food chain In-N-Out Burger is infamous for saying "no." Despite its fans begging the company to expand its operations to the East Coast, and despite its rapid growth and good reviews, the company has steadfastly refused. Several factors prevent the company from expanding. Since In-N-Out has no distribution facilities on the East Coast, expanding there would require freezing and then microwaving its food, which is at odds with the company's commitment to serving only fresh food. In-N-Out has thus chosen to maintain its high standards over meeting its customers' demands.

follow your passion

Some leaders have been stressed and unmotivated for so long that they have lost touch with their passion. They only see what's in front of them and plod forward from day to day. This impedes not only their own career progression, but also their teams' development. Who wants to report to someone who has very little passion for their work, leadership, or their employees?

What to do? Take time to reflect on how far you are from your areas of passion in your current job. Do you like your industry? Are you passionate about your products or services? Do you care deeply about your team or the people you work with? How about the company culture? Perhaps you've lost track of what your passion used to be. Try to remember what you used to dream about and enjoy. If you think you might be confusing lack of passion with burnout, reread the section on burnout in Chapter 3.

Finally, consider doing a career profile and perhaps a personality or leadership inventory. These tools will point you to where your passion and skills intersect. Engage an executive coach if you'd like additional support.

Talk with people who know you well and who have known you a long time. Do they recall times when you were less stressed and more motivated and passionate? What made you this way? Was it the people, the job, or the industry? Something else?

Passions do change over the life span of a career. Try to check in with yourself every few years. After all, there are people who will want to follow in your footsteps if they can.

You're probably going to be working a long time. Even if your career isn't lengthy, your work can easily take up to 50 percent of your waking hours (not counting commute time). It's much easier to stay motivated when you're passionate about your work.

Example in practice: I enjoyed my time as a CEO, but I knew that my passion for the next phase of my career was to learn new consulting skills and help a wider range of companies and industries. My current role as an executive consultant and coach allows me to fulfill that passion.

learn how careers are built

Everyone has preconceived notions about how successful careers are built. Many articles and blogs have been published stating, for example, that highly successful people wake up at 4:00 A.M. But there is no one-size-fits-all strategy when it comes to building a successful career. When leaders are stressed and unmotivated, their ambition evaporates, and they can become ineffective at forging good career paths. It's important to remember how careers are built, especially as your stress and motivation levels fluctuate.

What to do? A good initial stress solution is to select a few activities that interest, excite, and maybe even challenge you. When you lack motivation, you experience the same things day in and day out. The idea is to reignite your interest and expose yourself to new stimuli. Start small: Take a course in a new area or volunteer for a task force.

You can learn about people's career paths by looking on career websites. Better yet, do it face to face by interviewing five people in your company that are performing at high levels at their current jobs. Ask what motivates them. Ask them to share more about their background and how they prepared for their current role. Shadow them for half a day, and watch their strategies, tactics, leadership styles, and ways of learning. Compare this to your own work regimen. Is there anything you'd like to emulate?

Example in practice: Alibaba cofounder Jack Ma got off to a rocky start early in his career. He was rejected from 30 different jobs and turned down ten times applying to Harvard Business School. Ma persevered and ultimately decided to strike out on his own. He started to build websites for Chinese companies and gained invaluable firsthand experience in how to succeed in the internet age. Alibaba Group is now one of the largest ecommerce companies in the world.

When you're irritable, depressed, or anxious, it's easy to feel helpless. Helplessness, unsurprisingly, is one of the most ubiquitous emotional effects of stress.

helplessness

When you feel stressed and helpless, you don't feel in control. Many leaders and managers develop a condition called learned helplessness. *Learned helplessness* occurs when you are repeatedly subjected to an adverse effect that you have no control over. You may start to feel and act as if you are helpless to escape the situation. It becomes a vicious cycle, and you ultimately give up trying to regain control. What can you do to curb that feeling of helplessness?

get an assessment

Sometimes leaders are too close to a situation to see a solution. Sometimes they are too stressed and sensitive to the political dynamics at work, so they don't dare take a risk. Learn what the real situation is by turning inward and taking a self-assessment.

What to do? Invite an internal or external leader or team to conduct an assessment of the department, product, service, or situation. Sometimes the problem lies in whether you are hiring or promoting the right people. Sometimes it is caused by underestimating how complex an organization is. You will likely want to boil things down to their simplest form. But, especially in the workplace, things are often not as simple as they appear. It will take some time to understand the problem. Setting aside time to accomplish this will allow you to figure out how to move forward and out of your helplessness.

If you feel stuck at your company, try finding its movers and shakers. These are the people who get things done. They are the gatekeepers of information and can often supercharge your ability to navigate the organizational hierarchy, get buy-in, and overcome your helplessness.

Example in practice: The doctor's office down the street was referred to me. It became clear that the five physicians enjoyed taking care of patients, but the front desk operations were problematic. There was high employee turnover, office visit fees were not being reliably collected, they had received a letter from the city threatening to close the operation down, and the office manager was so exhausted that she couldn't seem to prioritize. I proposed an audit of the human resources and office systems and staff. It took me two weeks on-site to deliver an audit with two levels: "Do right now," and "do in three months." They were relieved to have items spelled out in a way the physicians and the office manager could follow. I did a post-audit after six months, and they were humming along like a Swiss watch. All it took was an HR specialist to perform a thorough assessment and provide some tools and actionable recommendations.

get your direct reports to perform

As a manager or leader, you have your hands full with your direct reports. But they're there to help you, too! Getting your direct reports to perform is a key way to reduce feelings of helplessness—both theirs and yours.

What to do? Don't be ambiguous when offering support and guidance to your direct reports. They won't perform well. Instead, create specific, measurable, achievable, relevant, and timely goals with your team members. Make sure your direct reports have a hand in deciding how to measure their progress; come to clarity together on the role, results, and criteria for success. Feel free to share all individual goals at a team level. Individual goals should be in direct alignment with the team's and your own (you can also share these). Transparency encourages teamwork and team support.

You should also give feedback to your employees. If they have areas of marked strength, recognize them. If there are areas in need of development, discuss them with your direct reports and offer training, mentorship, and online classes to help. Be sure to ask what their longer-term career goals are. Supporting the individual with care boosts trust and respect and flexes the skills on your team. Sure, this takes time. But you will feel less helpless because you will have a more engaged, dedicated, and skilled team to support you.

Make sure the performance standards are fair across your direct reports. This will help you build trust, gain buy-in, and avoid reluctance to perform within standards. If employees voice concerns, empower them and make sure you understand what their concerns are. Often, the people closest to the work are in the best position to assess and recommend standards or identify obstacles. This also combats helplessness.

Address poor performance quickly. Offer support and resources for your direct reports to improve within a certain time frame. If they don't improve, enlist HR and your own manager to help. Together, you should either decide on a plan to transfer the report to a position where he or she can succeed or recommend termination. If an employee violates a compliance or legal policy, bring in HR immediately and take notes for yourself at every step.

At staff meetings, send out agenda items in advance. Give everybody a chance to check in and talk, and take time to understand different viewpoints. Listen intently and with an open mind. Acknowledge you understand and take concrete actions. Make sure you follow up. This will encourage your direct reports to speak up and help ensure they buy in to your mission for a high-performing team.

Example in practice: As a big fan of visual management systems, I always encourage clients to have a board where key projects and performance indicators can be displayed. A few years ago, one of my clients, a large medical group, was struggling to recruit top physicians. I recommended that my client set up a board in the hallway to display the number of physician applicants, the costs, the time per hire, application channels, marketing efforts, and interaction with residency programs. The physicians enjoyed studying the board, and the leaders and employees felt empowered and recognized for their success.

stop procrastinating, start persisting

Feeling helpless and stressed can turn some of the best leaders into stone. Some people are just seasoned procrastinators by nature, putting off work until the very last moment. To reduce your feelings of helplessness as a leader, and to model good work habits for the people you work with, stop procrastinating and start persisting.

What to do? Divide your work into buckets. Book time to complete tasks into your calendar, and list the main actions to achieve the more complex tasks. Be realistic, and build in extra time (not for distractions, as you will have turned those off or blocked them, but for planning and thinking through your tasks). Chances are you'll underestimate the time required to complete work, which then makes you feel more helpless and stressed. Instead, fuel your persistence by setting small deadlines. For each chunk of the task, break it down into smaller pieces with clear milestones. You will feel more empowered and gain momentum and confidence. Consider what will happen when you face dependencies or obstacles. Map and schedule out those, too, so you don't get stuck in rabbit holes.

Example in practice: Elon Musk, CEO of Tesla, is famous for packing a lot into each of his days. How does he persist and avoid procrastination? Musk relies on a strategy known as time blocking. He follows a very strict schedule, planning out each of his days into five-minute increments. While this is an extreme approach, it illustrates the value of planning out each minute of your day.

increase your industry expertise

It's easy to get stuck in a rut in a company or industry, which can lead to narrow thinking and helplessness. One way to prevent this is to increase your industry expertise.

What to do? Join a conference board, which is a great outlet to share thoughts and bond over similar situations. Consider attending one of the national conference board meetings in your industry. Almost every industry has a national association. Join it. Meet industry peers, share experiences and learnings, and immerse yourself in your customers.

Example in practice: Many successful leaders, like Steve Jobs and Bill Gates, made a practice of getting in front of customers to better understand their businesses. Listen in on customer service calls or man the checkout counter. The experience and knowledge you gain will be priceless.

evaluate your workspace

It's easy to feel helpless and stressed when you are buried under mountains of work, literally and figuratively. If your work environment is distracting, cluttered, or chaotic, it can increase your feelings of helplessness. The best cure? Getting organized.

What to do? Take an inventory of your work space. Is your desk messy? Clean it up. Is your phone constantly ringing? Mute it or leave it on only during select hours. Do your direct reports cause you to have impromptu meetings? Try confronting them. These disruptions can quickly lead to a sense of helplessness. Decide what actions you need to gain control of your environment.

Example in practice: Some time ago, I noticed that one of the work space rentals I use had changed its model from open space to one with many more small offices and conference rooms. I used it for some of my larger, confidential client meetings, so I asked what was going on. They told me the change was in response to customer requests and rental patterns. People were moving away from open space offices because they were finding it too difficult to concentrate due to noise, proximity interruptions, and food smells. Clients were realizing that the loss of productivity cost them more than they saved by renting out the cheaper open space offices. Work space is important.

get periodic feedback

Everyone feels helpless at times. A key driver of helplessness is a lack of direction. If you're unsure whether you are doing a good job, it's easy to lose hope. As a leader especially, when there is often no recipe book for success, it's important to get periodic feedback.

What to do? Benchmark your progress with peers in your industry or your corporate function. Get some solid insight into how far they have come, either in terms of expanding and refining their products and services to customers or in terms of rising through the corporate ranks. For example, if you're in the real estate business, look at your competitors' numbers. How are they performing relative to the market? If your corporate function is finance, check out what different CFOs and controllers rely on in terms of the talent, internal service, tools, and efficiencies at their companies.

Looking for another way to get feedback? Find a person or a group of people you don't see every day, and explain the specific skill or competency from this book you are trying to use to reduce stress. Schedule check-ins with them for at least the midpoint and final date you hope to build the skill by, and ask them for raw and honest feedback on your progress. If you're firmly and authentically committed to building the skill, the periodic feedback will fuel your determination and ensure that you don't revert to a state of helplessness.

Example in practice: One of my clients is the executive director of an environmental organization that spends its days measuring the quality of air, land, and water in the San Francisco Bay. My client, having been in the job for five years, felt a little unsure about the impact of his organization's work. I suggested holding a fair that would be open to the public as an opportunity for the partnering agencies that use his organization's data to present their work. It turned out their cleanup and prevention work was astoundingly effective. The event was so successful that the mayor came to open it, and his employees, as well as the community, received a lot of powerful feedback. It is now an annual event. This type of periodic feedback can be a real morale booster.

If not dealt with, helplessness can quickly morph into depression. If high levels of stress cause you to feel depressed, this next section should be welcome reading for you.

depression

Depression is a severe feeling of sadness. You tend to lose hope, self-esteem, and interest in daily life. Activities you once enjoyed no longer bring you a sense of pleasure. But don't worry—there are a lot of solutions at your disposal. **Important:** If you are depressed and you feel like you want to hurt yourself, please tell a friend or loved one immediately and see a professional. Depression is common and treatable; you don't have to suffer needlessly.

avoid comparison

When you compare yourself to other people's careers, accomplishments, and lives (especially when you're stressed and depressed), it only decreases your self-esteem. Remember that a person's life can appear perfect on the outside, but you don't know what they are really feeling on the inside. It's important to avoid comparison.

What to do? Social media is often the worst offender when it comes to making comparisons. Consider taking a break from it. Suspend or disable your online accounts and take comfort in the fact that you're taking a stand against superficial pictures and posts. Intimate face-to-face conversations are a much better way of getting to know someone. By stepping inside their shoes, you're more likely to avoid making comparisons.

Example in practice: A marketing agency client of mine had a vibrant, positive culture. One director at the company, however, felt that another director was being given all the "interesting and fun" accounts. She complained loudly that she was stuck with the "stale and boring" accounts. The other director, tired of hearing about it, offered to switch accounts for six months. The complaining director quickly learned that the grass was not greener and that making comparisons was not helpful—in fact, it was misleading. The deeper lesson was that her own attitude accounted for a good chunk of her less impressive track record.

connect with one other leader

Isolation is closely tied with depression. As a leader, it's often most lonely at the top. Connecting with another leader can be a powerful way to ward off stress and depression.

What to do? Find a leader you admire and schedule weekly or biweekly coffee chats or walks. Share experiences, talk over challenging obstacles you're facing or questions you're pondering, and ask for their thoughts and advice. By sharing stories and lessons learned, you'll bond over the similarities in your situations and learn from each other. In doing so, your mood will be lifted, knowing that you are not alone. You might even invite a couple more leaders to join you over time.

Example in practice: Apple cofounder Steve Jobs and Oracle founder Larry Ellison found enormous comfort and value in their 25-year friendship. Even during the last days before Jobs' death, the two went for long hikes together. Both leaders had been suddenly thrust into the spotlight and experienced a lot of criticism. Through their friendship, they were able to reduce stress by sharing experiences, passions, and advice.

mentor an employee

Helping others takes you out of your self-rumination and gloom and helps both you and the other person appreciate what you have. Remember, you have to act like a leader even when nobody's looking, and even though you might be motivated by self-interest.

What to do? Take the time to mentor an employee or colleague. You can provide guidance not only to someone who works directly for you but also to employees with whom you may not have day-to-day interactions with. How? Initiate a cross-departmental mentorship program that is focused on broad-based initiatives and goals. Or mentor a colleague outside the office by providing support for a hobby or personal interest.

Example in practice: The most successful leaders recognize the value of making connections and mentoring. Consider Himani

Mishra, cofounder and CEO of Brand Radiator, a leading marketing company in Patna and Bangalore. She has explained that she relies on a "People First Approach"—be it for the employees, clients, or at home. Businesses or homes are created by people, and hence we must always share the stage of success with them and shoulder their needs. She's taken this advice to heart and invests a lot of time into developing strong relationships.

switch up your routine

When you do the same sort of work over a long period of time, it's easy to get bored, fall into a slump, and become depressed. It's all downhill from there. A key antidote against depression is to switch up your routine.

What to do? Do you work with the same people day in and day out? Do you have the option of changing that? At least on a temporary basis, switch up the people you work with. Try taking on a side project with another team. Being exposed to different personalities can be invigorating and provide a lot of support. New people are more likely to recognize your unique traits and abilities. They just might give you that pat on the back that will catapult you out of your depressed state.

Example in practice: When working with clients, I always try to work with a mix of new and current clients. I find the new ones are an especially forceful breath of fresh air. They help me maintain perspective and realize the positives in my work.

your emotional stress experiments

Now that you've had practice selecting experiments to prevent the cognitive impacts of stress as a leader, it's time to address the emotional impacts. Using Table 6.1 on page 129, list the emotional training activities you do on a regular basis as well as one or two new emotional activities you are committing to starting tomorrow or sometime in the near future. Remember to list when you will start and when you will stop. It is always easier to commit to a new

1. Emotional Problem	2. What I'm Doing Now	3. Experimental Stress Solution	4. Start and End Date	5. Results and Observations

TABLE 6.1 **emotional stress experiment log**

activity for one week than forever. Don't forget to enlist a friend for support and accountability.

To jog your memory, here are step-by-step instructions for how to complete this stress solution worksheet:

- *Emotional problem.* Describe the issue you are trying to solve.
- *What I'm doing now.* List how you've been trying to solve it.
- *Experimental stress solution.* Explain what new stress solution you will experiment with.
- *Start and end date.* List start and end dates of the new stress solution experiment.
- *Results and observations.* Write out the results of the experiment. Describe what you observed, what you learned, and any adjustments you might make in the future. Will you continue with this stress solution?

chapter wrap-up

Do you find yourself irritable around your friends, direct reports, or other colleagues? Do you frequently find yourself questioning what they're thinking? Do people tell you you're not listening to them? In this chapter, you've taken a major step toward exercising your emotional finger. You've selected one or two stress solutions to experiment with in order to enhance your emotional functioning. It's now time to move on to your third stress finger: the interpersonal finger.

chapter 7

the interpersonal finger

Stress impacts how you relate to others. When you are stressed, your focus tends to move inward. You overlook or deprioritize the people around you and how you interact with them. And when you don't have a clear direction or structure for how you want to engage others in your work or personal life, you can end up improvising, missing opportunities, alienating people, and wasting time.

stress-less leadership

As a leader who experiences stress directly and works with people who are stressed, keep in mind that positive and transformative relationships are key to your success. As you ascend higher in leadership at your company, your results are increasingly a reflection of others' success. How you engage, motivate, direct, and develop your teams and other people in the company determines your outcome, and how you and your teams connect with partners, vendors, and clients also dictates your results. These work relationships contain many touch points.

Organizational structures are increasingly complex: Most people are part of matrixed organizations, and some of your closest colleagues may be employed by another company and sometimes located overseas. All this makes it difficult to have personal and positive impacts, especially when stress is part of the equation.

Just like the other fingers you can use to wave away stress, there are solutions to address the interpersonal aspects of stress. In this chapter, you will read about and experiment with real-world solutions to interpersonal stressors.

Our interactions with others are defined by long-established values, perspectives, motives, and beliefs. So remember that the way you do things isn't necessarily the way other people do things. The way you talk with and about individuals and teams, how you select people for your team, the way you evaluate them, and the way you treat them are all highly individual. Do you address people when irritable? Do you come at people focused solely on what they can do for you? Or do you vary your approach depending on their moods, personalities, skill sets, and preferences?

In the workplace, your social capital contributes to your success. Social capital is the way people measure your worth in social circles, and it affects how far people will go out of their way to help you and be loyal to you and how much your opinion matters in the company. Positive and transformative relationships are key to your success.

Organizations depend on teamwork and healthy interpersonal relationships. The more you can have a positive impact on the individuals around you, the faster your career will accelerate. In the next section, you will learn more about solutions to the interpersonal impacts of stress.

relationships

Relationships form the foundation for new projects, pilot business initiatives, innovation, promotions, and success. It's a shame that stress can impact leaders' abilities to realize the value of relationships. Here are some stress solutions you can experiment with.

listen with your ears open

Listening is how you process information. Great listeners get more information from their conversations with leaders, boards of directors, peers, and direct reports. They also understand them at a deeper level and develop a stronger rapport. This boosts loyalty and belonging in the other person and strengthens your reputation as a good relationship builder. The impact is greater than most leaders realize—and it doesn't cost a cent!

What to do? Listen to your colleagues, customers, vendors, bosses, and industry leaders without interrupting them. Ask questions. Step into their shoes before assuming, judging, or making it about you. Make good eye contact. Maintain open body language, and nod to indicate that you understand. Occasionally take notes and paraphrase their points back to them so you can be sure you understand.

Listening with your ears open doesn't mean you allow your day to be hijacked by anyone who wants your attention. Talk about stress! Use your time strategically. For example, consider scheduling a meeting for 30 minutes, and make sure you have another meeting booked right after that one so you can't run long. Let attendees know how much time you have at the beginning of the meeting so it's not awkward at the close. This way, you can listen and value the relationship without letting it control your precious time.

Example in practice: Do not rush in to fix what you perceive to be a problem. I will always remember the time I heard a colleague was retiring and there was no celebration planned. I immediately jumped in to say we should plan something. I was wrong. The retiree didn't want a big celebration. She instead planned to reach out to people after a couple of months to have lunch individually and in small groups. That way she could really connect with them. She knew the value of relationships, and I learned the value of just listening.

build your relationships with management

Bosses don't just make or break your job—they can make or break your career. It's hard to imagine a more important force in your work life. Your boss or board of directors is responsible for your review, your raise, your employment, retirement, and your health benefits. Yet leaders often don't see the true value of those relationships due to stress. When you are stressed, you are apt to focus inward instead of relating strategically to others.

What to do? If you're looking to optimize your relationship with your boss or board, the first step is to understand them. What matters to them? What do they value, and what are their values? Observe, listen, and learn. Be blunt: Ask them what matters to them in their business role and in life. The next step is to remember what matters to them as you prioritize your projects and communications. Let's say you distribute a monthly report to them. Include the items that most interest them at the top; put any other items that they need to know in the middle, and group all remaining items at the end. Call or text them about urgent new developments that are of interest to them, and see how they respond.

Learn how they see the organization and your role in it and what matters to them in your work and in their own work. Leverage this valuable intel. How can you be most helpful to them? Do they need you for your innovation skills or to launch new lines of products and services? Do they need you to be a solid, middle-of-the-road thinker and performer, keeping all the trains on track? Or do they need you to give them the inside scoop on something? Perhaps all the above? What is your value to them? How can you attain higher value, status, or social capital?

Example in practice: A few years ago, I helped a solopreneur start what is now a million-dollar business. I own a part of her venture. To this day, she texts me when she acquires a particular French product that I cannot find locally. She understands me, and I will always remember her.

know yourself

It's difficult to truly connect with others and value relationships accurately if you're under stress and don't know yourself well. Getting a clear and complete picture of yourself and your progress will fuel your ability to build relationships.

What to do? In order to know yourself, you need feedback. As a manager and leader, you're likely to find that people are unwilling to give you honest feedback, especially negative feedback. But it is a gift. Go out of your way to request negative feedback. I have a client who explicitly tells her team, "Argue with me!" By doing so, she is trying to find the holes in her line of thinking. She wants to uncover her own blind spots.

Confidential feedback channels such as private 360-degree reviews are often an effective way to get negative feedback. Make an effort to solicit feedback from multiple sources. Diverse feedback will help ensure that all boxes are checked. And when it comes time to interpret and evaluate the feedback, ask a colleague or expert to help.

Don't be arrogant. When you're arrogant, you tend to overrate yourself and your abilities, and others tend to rate you less favorably than your more neutral counterparts. When you keep your arrogance in check, you're more likely to get an accurate assessment. Finally, don't be defensive. You'll get less feedback, and you'll be less effective at building strong relationships.

Example in practice: As an executive coach, providing accurate feedback to clients is an important part of the coaching process. This feedback is gathered from peers, superiors, and teams. It is a great opportunity to get ideas from colleagues on what is working and what needs work. Last week, I asked one client if she was aware that she had interrupted her colleagues 11 times during a meeting. She was astounded. The first step toward change is awareness.

always be learning

Learning is tough when you're stressed, and it's even harder when you feel all eyes are on you. Contrary to popular belief, people will want to relate to you more when they see you as humble and willing to learn new things. Your relationships will be stronger, too. People will be eager to share their expertise on something you are learning.

What to do? You can't assume people will think you're ready to learn. You need to emphasize that you are open to others and genuinely interested in what they have to say. A key way to demonstrate that you have an "always be learning" mentality is to be an early adopter of a technology, a process, or a skill. Pick up something new and mention to those around you how delighted you are to learn something. Or engage a coach, and let people know. I have a client, the COO of the largest retail company in the area, who is incredibly proud to be 6 percent fluent in French. After two years, she never misses a class with her tutor. Six percent might not seem like much, but she can say hello to me in my native language, so it's something.

Go one step further and train others. Building or supporting the internal learning organization is key to demonstrating your bias toward learning. Make sure you're courageous, humble, and endearing in your efforts. Demonstrating your hunger to learn can be contagious, igniting a fire that makes it easier for others to learn, too. The result is a continuous learning organization.

To take full advantage of your new bias toward learning for your career trajectory, determine what's important for your current and future jobs. Look at requirements and roles, and evaluate what skills are necessary or beneficial. But look out for blind spots, and don't assume you have all the answers. Understand your level of competency, and always have a model for evaluating whether you're skilled enough to apply your new learning in a new environment.

As a leader, encourage this in others, too, as it will strengthen their careers and your relationship with them.

Finally, volunteer for task forces. They are low-risk outlets for learning new skills and competencies. Task forces are great ways to gain exposure with other departments and divisions. By getting out of your niche, you'll start to see new connections and expand your perspective. Outside task forces can also lead to interesting and beneficial relationships as well as empowering communities and global markets.

Example in practice: Many of the world's most successful leaders have a strong bias toward learning. Take Warren Buffett, who has stated that the key to his success is his habit of reading 500 pages every day. His strong affection for learning keeps him humble, reminds him that he doesn't always have all the answers, and helps him build new competencies.

build political capital

Political capital (and here I am referring to politics at work, not on the world stage) is an extension of social capital. It allows you to exert influence and sway decisions. Building your political capital will help you reduce and prevent stress. Strive to become a leader with strong social and political capital.

What to do? When building capital, turn your attention outward. You're bound to encounter some roadblocks along the way. Organizations are rife with gatekeepers who can expedite requests— or block them. Learn who you can and can't rely on. Politically savvy leaders have a knack for reading people, stepping inside their shoes, and predicting how they will react. They see each individual as unique, requiring a different approach. Being sensitive to people also entails reading nonverbal cues. Gestures, tone of voice, and other nonverbal cues can be a window into a person's soul.

When building political capital, whether at your paid or volunteer work, don't make extreme proclamations about your value system from the get-go. This can exclude and offend people. There may be polarizing issues at play, such as the latest move from offices to cubicles or the hiring of a new CEO. Instead, embrace a wide view and hear people out, but be prepared to stand your ground when needed. If there are conflicts, try to keep them minimal and grounded in facts. Focus on the problem, not the person. Above all, be flexible. Create a plan, but don't write it in stone. Have contingency plans, and embrace change.

Example in practice: One of my longtime clients initially struggled with building her social capital. She cared deeply about her team, but she was stressed because she didn't have the political know-how to advance. She was invisible to senior management. On my suggestion, she bought a huge whiteboard for her office, used it to depict her strategic plans for product launches, and held a 30-minute open forum each week. At first, very few people showed up. But over time, it became so well-attended that her guest speakers included some of the most senior leaders at the company, earning her some solid social capital. She had always had good ideas, but she hadn't taken the time to put them into a concrete form.

Putting relationships first is one of several ways to enhance your interpersonal capabilities as a leader. Another hallmark of a skilled interpersonal leader is the ability to motivate.

motivation

Stress can make it challenging for leaders to connect with people. It can make you isolated or invisible. Some stressed leaders even drive people away. Fear not. There are ways to motivate people to partner with you and your team to achieve shared goals, even as you continue your quest to combat and prevent stress. The key is in how you approach them to make the ask.

manage the first three minutes

It's common knowledge that first impressions are important. You should always try to manage the first three minutes of a conversation, especially when meeting or interacting with someone whose assistance you hope to secure. The first three minutes set the tone.

What to do? Focus wholeheartedly on being approachable. Look, listen, and learn: Look people straight in the eyes. Listen to what they are communicating, and learn what is important to them. Turn off all devices that might distract you. Make other people feel they are in a safe and valuable space. The more secure they feel, the more likely it is they'll confide in you. When you're approachable, you're more likely to gain more information—and more important information. You're also more likely to build social capital that allows you to call on others for advice, feedback, support, and favors in the future.

Example in practice: My client was refused his third round of venture capital funding. This is not unusual, but in this case, it made no sense because the company was doing very well. I asked to sit in on a meeting with potential investors and was flabbergasted at what I saw. My client entered the conference room with his CFO on one side and his VP of products on the other. All three put their things down at one end of the conference table and talked amongst themselves before finally making their way over to the other side of the table to shake hands with the potential investors. I advised my client to stop doing this immediately. The meeting doesn't start when the meeting starts. The meeting starts as soon as people can see each other. First impressions are everything. I told him to also contact the previous investors to apologize. This changed the dynamic, and after a few months, one of them agreed to invest again.

care about direct reports

Caring for others is an important part of flexing your interpersonal finger. When you care for your team of direct reports, there's a domino effect. Often a manager's direct reports lead teams of their own, who either lead teams as well or deal with customers. When you kick-start this domino effect, you can spark a culture of caring at your company.

What to do? Caring does not mean bringing doughnuts to work once a year. Caring means listening. Whenever you interact with your direct reports, start by listening to them. Don't finish their sentences or abruptly cut them off. These behaviors quickly signal a lack of caring. Caring also involves being vulnerable. Disclose an interesting tidbit about yourself, even if it seems tangential to your work. When you reveal personal information, it makes you more relatable and encourages them to do the same. One anecdote is usually enough. Remember, you are there to engage with, build, and develop your direct reports, not indulge in a retrospective of all your hobbies, relatives, pets, and favorite foods.

Caring also means taking a vested interest in another person. Commit to knowing at least three career or non-work-related facts about each of your direct reports. Accept others' vulnerabilities. Don't judge. Don't try to agree or disagree. Just listen and understand. Don't give advice or propose solutions unless you're asked. Caring about your direct reports will put you in the top tier of bosses.

Caring also involves wonder, so be curious and ask questions. Be inclusive, but don't try to be equal in your treatment of them. Each of your direct reports is unique and should be treated as such. I often advise clients to make a spreadsheet listing how each member of their team likes to be appreciated. Some want a private thank-you note while others want a more public recognition with cake for all!

All that said, if your direct report is angry, frustrated, scared, or demotivated, don't don a therapist cap. Let people vent. Ask questions. Support them, and remind them about your company's employee assistance program (EAP), if there is one. Above all, show that you care. When you act disengaged or signal that you punt work to others without thinking, it can have a major impact. Caring in itself is a stress-buster and relationship builder. You will be valued and more likely to be called on to partner on projects or work in the future.

Finally, list your previous ten bosses on a sheet of paper and separate them into categories. List five bosses in the "he/she cared the least about me and other members of the team" category and the remaining five in the "he/she cared the most about me and other members of the team" category. Reflect on what each boss did to demonstrate that he or she did or did not care. Which boss would you be most likely to help today? Compare each to your current role as a manager.

Example in practice: Frank Blake, former CEO of Home Depot, cared deeply about his employees. He devoted hours each Sunday to write handwritten thank-you notes to employees at every level who had delivered great customer service. It's estimated that he wrote nearly 25,000 thank-you notes over his seven-year tenure! His deep care for his employees engaged, motivated, and inspired those around him.

develop others' skills and careers

What goes around comes around. As a manager and leader, you need to take the time to help develop others' skills and careers if you want them to help you in the future. Everyone wants to grow, develop, and advance.

What to do? First, you need to invest the time. Consider how many direct reports you have. You need to devote about eight hours per year per direct report outside of your typical job to develop them. If you have ten or more reports, this can be a hefty time investment, but it's worth it. Decide what commitments you might need to give up to make time to develop your direct reports. Next, make sure you assess them in a fair and accurate way. Assess their current strengths and limitations, evaluate their competencies, and ask for feedback. Schedule 360-degree feedback reviews about every two years. This type of holistic review can help reveal overlooked areas for potential advancement. Put together a development plan that is sound and grounded for all reports.

Direct reports need to be challenged to grow and develop in their roles. As a rule of thumb, 70 percent of a development plan should be devoted to job and task content; 20 percent should be devoted to people to study, listen to, or work with; and 10 percent should be devoted to gaining knowledge from courses and reading. This may not work for everyone. If one or more of your direct reports come from a disadvantaged background, more mentorship or access to resources may be required.

Decide which areas of your own job you can delegate to others. As long as a task is not critical to your role, you can pass it off to others to advance their own potential. Remember that development is not always a warm and safe place. New initiatives and projects can be frightening at first, especially if your boss previously led the project.

Direct reports must be challenged to take on stressful tasks that expand their abilities. Help them learn by engaging in a learning dialogue and asking them to reflect on what they have learned. Ask them to step outside their comfort zone by inviting them to reflect on the benefits of development. Explain the purpose and value of each effort. Finally, help them expand their prospects by suggesting that they attend meetings run by other functional groups and creating opportunities that help them expand their perspectives.

Example in practice: When my clients are asked by their bosses to work with me, many initially see development as a waste of time. Sometimes they feel too insecure to develop their direct reports out of fear that someday those reports will surpass them. But talent incubators are responsible for shaping powerful leaders. They create the Warren Buffetts, Bernard Tysons, and Cathy Engelberts of the world, who in turn build strong, effective, dedicated, and loyal people who rush in to help or partner with them.

share a part of yourself

A key part of your ability to attract people who will help you in times of need is your willingness to share parts of yourself with others. People with strong interpersonal skills tend to share freely with others. Sharing is a gift that often leads to others sharing in return.

What to do? The next time you see someone struggling in their role, take a minute to step inside their shoes. Can you help them in any way? Give them a piece of advice or a tip that can help them boost their performance. If you've faced a similar situation, share your experience. If you haven't, imagine you have, and reflect on what it might feel like.

Example in practice: Some of the most successful leaders are adamant about openly sharing important details of their personal and professional lives, even when it might be difficult. In 2014, Apple CEO Tim Cook wrote a beautiful essay revealing he was gay. In writing the article, he knew there were risks involved—at the time he was the only openly gay CEO in the Fortune 500. But Cook recognized that hiding a fundamental part of himself was not going to help fix the lack of equality in the world. In giving up some of his privacy, he gave many people a role model to emulate.

take action

Nobody likes a passive or checked-out colleague, leader, or business partner. Yet this is precisely what stress and inaction can reduce leaders to. "Just do it" should be your mantra, whatever "it" means to you.

What to do? To take action, you need to stop procrastinating. Procrastination is the enemy of forward movement. If you're a procrastinator, take steps to avoid the trap of putting things off. Start earlier; set timed performance targets, and break your work into smaller manageable parts.

Perhaps, in addition to being a procrastinator, you are a perfectionist. If you're always seeking out perfect solutions, this can prevent action. Try to reduce your perfectionist tendencies. Embrace ambiguity. Taking action requires a high level of confidence. If you constantly second-guess your abilities, you need to build your confidence. Take a class or work with a coach to gain leadership competencies. Embrace your strengths and figure out how to use them to your advantage. When you've gained enough confidence, establish a set of best practices for organizing your week. Be diligent about your work ethic and habits.

Don't be afraid to recruit others. To take action, you sometimes need to rally some troops. But make sure you don't delegate all your work to them. The whole point is for you to do something for somebody else. Work on building your social capital and persuading others to join you. Finally, taking action involves an honest understanding of your commitment level. It's great to have work-life balance, but try to be flexible if it means helping others.

Example in practice: Many successful leaders procrastinate. It's said that Leonardo da Vinci took more than 15 years to complete the *Mona Lisa*! Like da Vinci, Instagram cofounder Kevin Systrom has struggled with procrastination and relies on a time-tested tactic to cope with it. Whenever he's having trouble getting started on something, he commits to doing at least five minutes of it. Once he gets over the initial hump, he's much more motivated to finish.

stand for a personal cause

Social causes and volunteer work are powerful stress busters and stress preventers. What's more, when people identify with a cause, they will go out of their way to help the individuals or companies that stand behind it. I was pleasantly surprised to learn that two clients selected me for their projects because I donate 100 percent of the proceeds of my books to the care and protection of animals.

What to do? Communicating your experience and values is key. If you want to be received favorably, make sure to explain *why* you have a certain belief or value rather than merely stating it as fact. Perhaps a trip to the Sudan led you to donate to Oxfam to combat hunger. Or perhaps after realizing your assistant had been living in her car for a year, you decided to advocate for affordable housing in your city (this happened to one of my clients). Finally, be sensitive to your audience. Start small and gradually build up the amount of disclosure, and you'll be on your way to standing confidently for a personal cause.

Example in practice: Several forward-thinking companies have committed themselves to a personal cause. Consider Toms. CEO Blake Mycoskie is focused on giving back to the global community by embracing a one-for-one model. Every time a customer purchases a pair of Toms shoes, the company donates a product or service to someone in need: shoes, eyeglasses, childbirth training, bullying prevention, clean water, and more. In 2018, Mycoskie committed to donate $5 million in support of ending gun violence. Being so invested in the community has escalated Toms' brand and given it a more human touch that people admire. It has a direct effect on the bottom line.

But the most effective leaders don't just motivate others around them. They go further and galvanize others to reach higher levels of performance.

performance

Stress contributes to low performance at the individual, leadership, and organizational levels. It also makes relationships more difficult to maintain. This can quickly lead to a situation where leaders are stressed, isolated, and perform poorly. No one wants to report to this kind of "leader." But don't worry—here are some stress solutions for you to experiment with.

select and hire talent

Knowing when to hire talent, what kind of talent to hire, where to find it, and how to select it takes time and organization, and those are often the first things to go when leaders are stressed. This can lead to poor performance across the organization. Commit yourself to becoming an expert at selecting and hiring talent.

What to do? Identify where the talent is. Talent entails much more than a high IQ. Always be on the lookout for talent inside and outside the company. Events, social gatherings, and conferences are great lookout spots. Ask your peers for recommendations, and look beyond the things that might appear on a resume. Ask experts for guidance on the best practices for selling the opportunity or company. Some stressed-out leaders can inadvertently chase talent away because they don't know how to present their company.

Embrace effective interview practices and psychological profiles. Adopt a validated method to screen talent and use a clear and consistent methodology for interviews. You should also ensure that there are purposeful onboarding and acculturation processes for new hires to help them become effective at their new jobs more quickly.

Ask your HR business partner to share an example of an agreed-upon talented individual, including core competencies related to performance. Take notes, make sure you understand, and map out what talent you need to realize short- and long-term objectives and results.

Looking for another stress solution? Make sure you have developed strong leaders who cultivate strong leaders in their own right. Show interest in your direct reports' high-performing employees, and ensure they are in the right role in the company. Make sure you have one or two successors that can step up and serve as your replacement. Surround yourself with talent. If some of them end up advancing further than you, that means you've done your job in finding and bringing on the right people. Kudos to you.

Example in practice: Shoe company Zappos is known for prioritizing selecting and hiring the right talent. It goes so far as to offer a "Pay to Quit" program, in which it pays new hires to quit! Why? Zappos wants to make sure its employees are passionate about the business. If new hires aren't swayed to leave by money, chances are they are in it for the long term and committed to honoring the company's values.

motivate and mobilize humans

Stress often prevents leaders from taking the time to motivate and mobilize people across their organization, causing engagement to plummet and impeding performance.

What to do? There are several management fundamentals associated with inspiring others. Follow their basic tenets, such as using goals, milestones, and rewards to motivate employees and teams. During your one-on-ones, tell your reports, especially your highest performers, that you support them in their growth plans and career ambitions. Provide tangible rewards, including a bonus or spot award if you can. Turn skills deficits or organizational negatives into motivators by transforming them into clearly defined challenges with rewards. For a large project, consider assigning a project or change manager to it as well. Make sure you add ample access and support to ensure that high-potential and high-performing employees gain new skills.

People respond to challenges in vastly different ways. It's important to find out what drives each person. To figure this out, look for what they emphasize in conversation. Do they focus on certain events or people? These can reveal powerful motivational forces. Or ask them directly, but make sure you can speak their language. This will make it easier for them to open up to you. Now that you've entered their world, let them enter yours. They need to know how you think and the reasons behind your actions.

Example in practice: Last year, I was referred to a client who was described as "a genius but low-performing tech leader." The leader's manager sent him to me to "fix him." I assigned him my full battery of business and personality tests and performed his 360 review. It all came out fine, and we did great work together. He ended up clinching a promotion in a different department. This led me to one conclusion: The referring manager could use some help motivating and mobilizing humans. Needless to say, I called him up, and he agreed to let me coach him.

build strong teams

When stressed, executives can be so focused on other things that they overlook the importance of ensuring that their direct reports are building skilled, strong teams. And yet building high-performing teams across the organization is critical to the company's success, the employees' careers, and preventing stress. Nobody wants to report to a boss who is stressed and not performing, and whose boss is also stressed and not performing.

What to do? Get everyone on the same page by establishing a common cause for your team or organization as well as a shared mindset (such as company values). This can be communicated in town hall meetings, calls, incentive compensation plans, and events. There are entire books devoted to building strong teams. In this book, I highlight only the areas that crumble under stressed leaders.

Another stress solution involves establishing and communicating key performance indicators to increase clarity across your team or company. When everyone is on the same page, it's much easier for the collective to focus and reach their peak potential. Every few years, review or create an organizational structure and make sure all efforts are complementary and no work is duplicated. If you are the CEO of a large company, you might bring in a consulting firm to assist with strategic and operational roles, expected outputs, and compensation plans. Under stress, leaders tend to forget to develop leaders who build strong teams.

At all times, remember to inspire, support, and develop your team, and expect them to do the same for their own teams. Tell them directly and through your actions that you value them and the people who report to them. Tell them that their work is important. *Don't* go around your leaders and micromanage their direct reports; empower them to handle their teams directly. *Do* set up skip-level meetings once a year to spot trends and high performers.

Finally, conduct formal talent reviews and succession planning. You can do this yourself or enlist the help of a consultant or Human Resources team. Reward leaders with the highest-performing and most potential talent on their teams. Hire and promote from within as much as possible. Have a strong, vibrant leadership academy, and create a breeding ground for experimentation and innovation. Creativity is a propeller of stronger teams. Celebrate experiments and out-of-the-box thinking.

Example in practice: Fostering an environment that fuels creativity is critical to building a strong team. Consider Ben & Jerry's. The famous ice cream company has a reputation for concocting outrageous ice cream flavors with widespread appeal. It owes a lot of its success to its focus on creating a psychologically safe environment. To encourage out-of-the-box thinking, it built a "Flavor Graveyard" at its Waterbury, Vermont factory to honor the company's failed ice cream flavors. Unsuccessful flavors are celebrated rather than swept under the rug. This type of low-risk environment fuels creativity and innovation.

have difficult performance conversations

Most people don't enjoy critical conversations, and the ones about low performance are particularly tough. Ironically, these situations require you to subject yourself to more stress in order to feel less stress.

What to do? It's easy to assume that poor performers know they aren't living up to their potential. But in reality, many of them don't. Feedback is a gift. Don't wait for someone to veer completely off course. Help them realize the gaps between their actual performance and their expected performance. If your team members don't know how they'll be evaluated, they're likely to fall short. It's your job to outline key results areas and indicators of success. These performance standards will help you avoid surprises when having difficult performance conversations.

Whenever you're getting ready to have one of these conversations, map out a possible improvement plan. Don't be critical without proposing a solution. It's your job to sit down with the employee and lay out actionable steps to improve performance. This plan can involve tactics such as additional training, or it can involve stopping or starting certain behaviors. Finally, know when to cut ties. If an employee truly isn't able or willing to perform up to standards, propose a better job fit or role where the person can succeed. Everyone has strengths.

Example in practice: I've learned that the leap from director to vice president is often a larger challenge than leaders plan for. A CEO called me recently because he was facing this exact issue. Fortunately, he was experienced and skilled at having difficult conversations to achieve good performance, and I was able to immediately jump in and coach his new vice president to success.

coach a direct report or colleague in uncharted territory

Sometimes high-potential talent is thrown into a new job without the necessary criteria to be effective. It's tempting for them to follow their gut reaction when trying to solve a problem and lean on tactics that worked for them before. Sometimes they are stubborn; other times, they're just confused. This is a vulnerable time for them. You can make a big positive impact on their career and mental health by acting as their coach as long as you take a strategic approach to it.

What to do? Don't just listen to them vent. Invite them to start by listening and not talking. Suggest they act as if they've been planted in an alternate universe so everything they thought they knew is irrelevant.

Tell them to first try to fully define the problem. Consider talking to people, asking questions, and looking for experts and people who have some knowledge of the job, local market, or region. Let them know it's best to be patient with ambiguity and not having all the answers. Urge them to avoid jumping to conclusions, taking action, or giving direction.

These ventures into uncharted territory, especially if it is a new country, can make for fascinating storytelling. More than that, though, the person you are coaching will forever see you as a lifeline in the madness of the jungle.

Example in practice: I once worked with a client who got promoted beyond her capabilities. By the time she and I started working together, she was failing in her role as a manager because she didn't take the time to learn the environment or the people. With some coaching, she was able to take a more strategic approach to her new job and improve her assessment, learning, and ability to connect to others.

It's not enough for leaders to focus on enhancing the capabilities of existing talent, however. They must also work to retain this talent while attracting new talent.

talent management

Stress impacts a leader's ability to invest in their interpersonal relationships. If this permeates through the leaders' teams and the company, the brand suffers. If leaders don't connect to employees, employees don't connect to customers, and the brand takes a nosedive. You want an internal and external brand that is synonymous with trust and high quality. Fortunately, there are many solutions to leverage.

manage nonverbal cues

Most of your interpersonal conversation is nonverbal. If you're bent on exercising your interpersonal finger, make an effort to better understand nonverbal communication.

What to do? Whenever you're interacting with another person, take note of your body language. Are you slumped over or standing tall? Also consider your tone. Are you speaking angrily and causing others to recoil? Are you using annoying office or slang buzzwords? Are you using too few words to develop a connection with others? Or are you using so many as to incite boredom?

You'll also want to pay attention to the company's reputation vs. what they say in marketing campaigns. When candidates' and employees' experiences at work don't match the rhetoric, they instantly distrust leaders and the company. Since they have choices, employees will go elsewhere. It's important to be congruent across all channels, including your website (and the images on it), branding, marketing campaigns, and social media. Of course, the company's corporate citizenship and contributions to society also matter to candidates and employees. Granted, it's hard to even think about these issues if leaders are overstressed or unskilled at attracting or retaining talent.

Example in practice: My financial services client was having a tough time hiring analysts on the risk side of their business, so they called me in to find out why. I found that the prestigious global finance firm was any new candidate's dream. The salary was great, the perks were appealing, and recruiters were always flooded with quality applicants. But the risk analysts turned the offer of employment down 65 percent of the time compared to 5 percent across the rest of the firm.

I was at a loss until I sat in on an interview. The hiring manager asked all the right questions, reading them straight from HR's interview sheet. But his lack of eye contact and snippy tone revealed him as self-centered, uninterested, and in a mad rush. Body language? He ate a burger and slurped his diet soda loudly during the interview, even knowing I was there to audit the process. I attached a photo to my report, and he insisted on posing next to a picture of himself bungee jumping hamburger in hand. His nonverbal cues told me everything I needed to know. A deep follow-up conversation led him to reflect and realize the effects of his behavior. He jumped at the opportunity to engage me as a coach.

foster inclusion

When you're stressed, your brain seeks out familiarity and sameness. Nobody wants to work for a leader who is not inclusive and who can't attract or retain talent. As a leader, attracting and retaining talent is important because it allows your career to progress and enables the organization to flourish.

What to do? The first step toward managing diversity is to provide equal opportunities across the board. Equal opportunity does not mean equal treatment—it means differential treatment with a focus on inclusion and diversity. To attract and retain all kinds of talent, you must be willing to make adjustments to level the playing field. Some team members, teams, or even offices may need additional mentorship, training, or simply more recognition.

In addition to embracing equal opportunity, you need to be aware of differences and whether they impact performance. Don't assume that a particular group is destined for subpar performance. Don't pigeonhole people. Be aware of your own unconscious biases. Better yet, take an unconscious bias training course. When you can understand people without first judging them, you'll find yourself managing diversity.

Finally, it will be hard to manage diversity if there isn't much diversity in your own life. Make a conscious effort to interact with people from different backgrounds. Visit different cultural events in your own town, or travel to new regions in the world.

Example in practice: After a very public incident involving race discrimination against a couple of customers, Starbucks sent 175,000 of its employees to a one-hour unconscious bias training program. A quick dive like this will probably not move the needle on conscious or unconscious bias, however. I took a different and deeper approach with a client of mine who provides pharmacy products. We provided education by the team members themselves in an interactive and empowering format. And for career, development, health, and wealth impact, we weaved in equalizing processes and tools at these junctions: hiring, orientation, performance, training, cultural events, benefits, and separation.

practice good interpersonal skills at all levels

Employee and customer care can go straight out the window when you are stressed, and it shows in how you treat others. This can lead to poor attraction and retention of talent. Focus on your day-to-day personal interactions with colleagues at all levels of your organization.

What to do? Teach and model daily interactions that are considerate, polite, and inclusive. Many people join organizations as their first job or come from companies with very different cultures. Establishing a warm, collaborative environment depends on all employees using key words at key times. These can be taught at vendor and employee orientations as well as customer service and management training, and can be referred to and reinforced periodically. Words, questions, and statements like "Hello," "Good morning," "Is now still a good time?", "I am sorry for the confusion," "Thank you for your time," or, "Have a wonderful day," can make all the difference. You feel it right away when you walk into this type of environment. I find that my clients in health care and hospitality have employees who rely on this approach, probably because their business depends on it. On the flip side, some of my clients have employees who are glued to their devices and isolated from their peers. It's always preferable to have a team with good interpersonal skills because, for the most part, people like to shop and work at a company where nice behavior is the norm.

Good interpersonal skills are also flexible. Every person is different, with different values, motivators, skills, and triggers. Embrace differences and try to adapt to other people's ways of doing things. The crux of successful interpersonal skills lies in your ability to be savvy both with people you like and people you don't like. When interacting with the latter, try to establish a place of common interest. Don't judge or make rash assumptions. Try to talk less, listen more, and ask more questions.

Example in practice: In 2014, Facebook CEO Mark Zuckerberg surprised a large Chinese audience by speaking in Mandarin. Few knew he had been taking classes in the language for years. Zuckerberg's motivation to learn Mandarin was undoubtedly driven by his longtime desire to capitalize on China's 1 billion-plus population. Regardless, he became an instant celebrity because he had made an effort to learn Chinese culture and language.

communicate and live by values

As a stressed leader, it can be tough to focus on attracting and retaining talent by communicating and living by your values. It seems like there is just so much else to do. In reality, people are looking for bosses and co-workers with good values who will treat them well.

What to do? When it comes to values and ethics, there's sometimes a disconnect between what leaders say, what their values should be, and what they actually do. Reflect on what you say your values and ethics are. Then give a few examples of times you've demonstrated them. Is there a disconnect? If so, it's time to either change your values or model your current ones more effectively.

Looking for another stress solution to experiment with? Managers and leaders have a responsibility to convey the importance of their values and ethics to their teams. Consider writing down your value system so that it's concrete. Think about your recent actions in different areas, including delegation, spending, resource allocation, hiring, and performance reviews. Did you model certain ethics and values? Was it consistent? Do you want to be remembered for modeling these ethics and values? When you the take the time to reflect on what you say your values are and what you actually do, you'll be able to determine if there's a disconnect. The more alignment there is, the more effective you'll be at conveying the importance of values to your team.

Example in practice: Many leaders have been criticized for publicly saying they endorse certain values and then doing something vastly different in practice. Facebook has come under much scrutiny for this. In March 2018, it was revealed that Facebook knew about massive data theft and did nothing about it. This signaled that the company did not prioritize "building social value," which is one of its core values. When there's a disconnect between words and actions, brand strength takes a nosedive.

your interpersonal stress experiments

You're a pro now! It's time to address the interpersonal impacts of stress. Using Table 7.1 on page 156, list the interpersonal training activities you do on a regular basis, as well as one or two new interpersonal activities you are committing to starting tomorrow or sometime in the near future. Remember to list when you will start and when you will stop. It is always easier to commit to doing a new activity for one week than forever. Don't forget to enlist a friend for support and accountability.

To jog your memory, here are step-by-step instructions for completing the stress solution worksheet in Table 7.1:

- ▸ *Interpersonal problem.* Describe the issue you are trying to solve.
- ▸ *What I'm doing now.* List how you've been trying to solve it.
- ▸ *Experimental stress solution.* Explain what new stress solution you will experiment with.
- ▸ *Start and end date.* List the start and end dates of your new stress solution.
- ▸ *Results and observations.* Write out the results of the experiment. Describe what you observed, what you learned, and any adjustments you might make in the future. Will you continue this stress solution?

1. Interpersonal Problem	2. What I'm Doing Now	3. Experimental Stress Solution	4. Start and End Date	5. Results and Observations
Interrupting	Telling myself not to before meetings.	Alice will touch her ear each time I interrupt so I become aware.	Monday 6/6 to Friday 6/11.	I am catching myself before Alice touches her ear. I am interrupting once or twice per meeting. Down from 20 times. I see it's about trying to rush the agenda because I'm stressed about my emails piling up as I'm in the meeting.

TABLE 7.1 **interpersonal stress experiment log**

chapter wrap-up

As this chapter closes, let's take a minute to talk about the leader's interpersonal life. The higher a leader is in the organization, the more public her life is. With social media, mapping, and surveillance

---

a note about colleagues and cultures

Choose who you work with and evaluate the company culture wisely. Sometimes less-reputable people are attracted to certain fields or industries and become experts and leaders within them. This doesn't mean you can't choose who you work with. You spend most of your working days with your co-workers. Seventy-eight percent of employees who clock 30 to 50 hours per week spend more time with their colleagues than with their families.[1] Your relationships with your co-workers affect your well-being and your opportunities for advancement. So choose carefully.

---

technology, there is very little privacy or expectation of it. Your reputation affects your career trajectory.

But humans are social animals; even introverts need people. There's a reason isolation is a common form of torture. Your social relationships have a remarkable impact on your health and stress levels. You owe it to yourself to strengthen them. The health of your social support networks also has a hefty impact on your stress levels. Positive social support increases resilience to stress. You've probably noticed that your stress levels tend to decrease when you're laughing with, and surrounded by friends.

Developing strong social connections in and outside the workplace is key to successful leadership. Research has shown that a combination of a strong results orientation and social ability characterizes the most successful leaders.[2] Leaders with strong social skills can motivate their team to achieve peak performance; maintain supportive, collaborative relationships; and combine the complementary strengths of individual team members. In effect, they ensure that the whole is greater than the sum of the individual parts.

As a leader, it's critical to develop strong social skills and personal relationships. Schedule enough time with friends, family members, and co-workers. Prioritize face-to-face interactions. A lack of social ties can induce tremendous stress. By focusing on developing quality relationships, leaders increase their engagement skills and ignite a friendlier, healthier culture at work. Social relationships also reduce personal stress levels and help people lead happier lives.

Now that you've developed a game plan to build your interpersonal capabilities, you're well on your way to becoming a more effective leader. In the next chapter, you'll learn how you can start to enhance your fourth stress finger—the physical finger.

chapter 8

the physical finger

*a*s you learned in Chapter 1, stress causes a hodgepodge of different physical effects, including muscle tension, headaches, migraines, diabetes, and strokes. The good news is that by exercising your physical finger, you can minimize, prevent, or even reverse the negative physical effects of stress.

Leadership is rife with obstacles and challenges. It requires tremendous endurance, stamina, and mental strength. By better understanding the components of your physical finger, you can enhance your effectiveness as a leader and improve your focus, alertness, mental agility, and—ultimately—performance. In this chapter, you'll learn about the physical foundations of peak leadership performance: exercise, diet, and sleep. I have structured this chapter a bit differently from the other "finger" chapters to include some of the science behind these physical factors, so you'll see a few sidebars and extended section introductions. Let's start by taking a look at the physical finger components in Figure 8.1 below.

Let's start with a quick quiz. Rank each of the following components of the physical finger according to how much you prioritize them (with "1" indicating highest priority and "3" indicating lowest priority).

Physical Component	Priority Level (1-3)
Exercise	
Diet	
Sleep	

All three components of your physical finger are essential to your ability to lead. Reflect on which aspect you ranked "3" in priority. As you read this section, you'll likely want to pay close attention to this component. Chances are you're not devoting enough time to addressing it.

FIGURE 8.1 **quiz: physical finger components**

exercise

Physical activities act as the fourth finger in combatting stress. Exercise is an important component of your physical finger. It generates new cells and blood vessels in the brain and can increase the volume of white and gray matter in the brain.

The highest performing leaders know the importance of incorporating exercise into their daily routines. Your cognitive capacity is directly linked to your physical fitness. Exercise is associated with increased concentration, enhanced memory, faster learning, improved mood, and even enhanced creativity.

It's common knowledge that exercise is good for the brain. Indeed, the relationship is well-supported by research. A 2008 study from the University of Bristol found that employees who visited the gym during the workday were more productive and had smoother interactions with colleagues compared to employees who abstained from exercise.[1] Gym-bound employees also left work feeling more satisfied at the end of the day.

A key to reducing your stress levels is physical exercise. This includes adopting a healthy exercise regime incorporating both aerobic and bone density activities. Let's look at what you can do.

incorporate aerobic activity

Aerobic activity gets your heart going. It is vital for heart health and gives you that critical endorphin boost. Jogging, moderate walking, biking, dancing, and swimming are all wonderful sources of aerobic activity that you can do indoors or outdoors.

What to do? Commit to doing one aerobic activity for a minimum of 20 minutes at least three times a week. Choose something you'll enjoy rather than dread. I like to incorporate my meditation with my exercise, walking and contemplating. You may choose to do the same. Over time, you'll find that you'll lower your heart rate, blood pressure, and stress levels.

Example in practice: Countless successful leaders credit part of their success to exercise. Consider Richard Branson, founder of the Virgin Group. He's religious about starting each day with an aerobic activity. He avoids monotony by mixing it up: tennis, biking, kitesurfing. Sounds exciting! And stress quelling.

work on your bone density

Exercise plays an important part in helping you maintain and even improve your bone density. When you exercise, you increase the size and strength of your muscles, and the force of the muscles pulling against bone strengthens your bones as well. Bones are active and living, just like you, and living things only adapt when they are placed under stress. Don't worry, your body will love you for it.

What to do? Choose a high-impact weight-bearing activity to do twice a week for at least 20 minutes each session. Great options include push-ups, pull-ups, lifting weights, planks, jumping rope, and climbing stairs.

Example in practice: I've long appreciated the joy of incorporating aerobic dance and weights into my physical fitness regimen. The music is international and inspiring, and I love moving and getting my pulse up. I often lift weights right after class since I am already warmed up.

diet

While the brain composes 2 percent of total body weight, it consumes about 20 percent of the total energy that the body gets from nutrients. It should come as no surprise that a healthy diet is linked to lower levels of stress. Diets low in sugar, for example, increase *brain-derived neurotrophic factor* (BDNF), a peptide responsible for the creation of new neurons. BDNF plays a critical role in neuroplasticity, as it allows neurons to connect and combine.

High-fiber foods such as whole grains and legumes help keep blood sugar levels stable, which also has an impact on how the body handles stress. They have a low glycemic index and are digested slowly. Nuts are known to be heart-protective and contain many antioxidants. Walnuts are especially health-promoting and are a rich source of omega-3 fatty acids, which can lower heart disease risk and reduce total cholesterol and LDL (bad cholesterol). Diets high in fruits and vegetables have also been shown to reduce the risk of developing certain cancers. You can take a quick quiz on fiber content in Figure 8.2 on page 163.

In addition to fiber, carbohydrates are an important component of your diet. Carbohydrates increase your serotonin levels, which help enhance your mood and reduce stress. Whole grain bread or

This one's a tough one. Rank the following fruits according to their level of fiber content (with "1" indicating the highest level and "4" indicating the lowest level).

Fruit	Rating (1-4)
1. 1 medium apple with skin on	
2. 1 medium orange	
3. 1 cup of raspberries	
4. 1 medium pear	

Solutions: 1. "3," 2. "4," 3. "1," 4. "2"

FIGURE 8.2 **quick quiz: fiber content**

pasta can significantly enhance your cognitive functions, making you more alert, focused, and productive.

Another essential component of a stress-quelling diet is omega-3 fatty acids. Omega-3s help stabilize the adrenal hormone and can prevent it from rising too high during bouts of intense stress.

Many people crave sugar in response to stress, but a diet high in refined sugars can greatly enhance stress levels. Refined sugars release glucose quickly into the bloodstream, which in turn causes insulin to be released to help absorb the excess glucose and stabilize blood sugar. This makes your blood sugar levels fluctuate and ultimately causes your emotions and moods to fluctuate as well. The result is that you're more inclined to react adversely to stress.

You may be surprised to learn that vegan diets can also enhance emotional health. A 2015 study found that vegans reported lower levels of stress and anxiety as compared to vegetarians, who, in turn, reported lower levels of stress compared to omnivores.[2] The researchers suggested that animal fats may activate inflammatory pathways in the brain that are responsible for stress. Although not investigated in the study, the guilt and shame of hurting and killing animals is also another hard-hitting effect for many people.

Even if you're not willing to jump on the vegan bandwagon, incorporating leafy greens into your diet can be a great antidote against stress. Kale, collards, and spinach are especially effective at reducing inflammation caused by stress. They are rich in several essential nutrients and minerals such as B vitamins that help regulate your mood.

No matter how you choose to address your diet, it's important to furnish your body with the right food and nutrients. This fuel affects not only your physical stamina, but also your mental stamina. Here are some solutions to try.

maintain a healthy diet

You've already learned about how foods affect your stress levels. Now it's time to put your knowledge to good use. Maintaining a healthy diet is key to your ability to reduce stress. A healthy diet need not be restrictive.

What to do? Ensure that you are consuming a variety of foods. This will ensure you're getting a good mix of critical nutrients and supplements. Look at the ingredients. If you notice that any critical nutrients are missing, add a supplement to your diet. Keep an eye on your portions to ensure you're not overeating. That supersized hamburger can easily throw your efforts off-course. Try to reduce or eliminate meat whenever possible. Be sure to incorporate at least two-and-a-half cups of vegetables and two cups of fruit a day into your diet. Aim to increase whole grains and minimize added sugar.

Example in practice: There are many well-known leaders in their fields who are vegan. While Woody Harrelson initially ditched animal products decades ago for health reasons, it seems the actor then became increasingly interested in the ethical principles behind the lifestyle. In 2017, Harrelson appeared in a thought-provoking video alongside fellow vegans Sir Paul McCartney and Emma Stone. The video addressed the ethical and environmental issues surrounding animal agriculture and urged viewers to reduce their meat intake.

sleep

Sleep is another important component of your physical finger. Everyone needs their zzz's. One 2016 study found that sleep resets the connections in the brain that are crucial for memory and learning.[3] Lack of sleep causes the brain's neurons to become so "muddled" with electrical activity that memories can't form properly. The loss of a single night's sleep is enough to disrupt the brain's natural reset mechanism. Check your sleep efficiency in Figure 8.3 below.

Let's get real about sleep. It's important. Answer the following statements according to whether they are true ("T") or false ("F").

Statement	True ("T") or False ("F")
I have difficulty falling asleep.	
I get the required 7 to 9 hours of sleep each night.	
I feel rested when I wake up.	
I have a consistent bedtime.	

If you answered "T" to three out of four statements, you're well on your way to developing healthy sleep habits. If not, there's lots of room for improvement. This section contains a gold mine of information for you to leverage.

FIGURE 8.3 **quiz: your sleep efficiency**

As an executive, you may be highly susceptible to sleep deprivation, and its effects can be devastating. Your cognitive processes are impaired. Your irritable mood affects your relationships, and your decision-making abilities deteriorate.

Sleep is an essential stress queller and a precious time to rejuvenate and restore your mind and body. It gives your body time to heal and empowers you to wake up and tackle the day. Here's what you can do to enhance your sleep efficiency.

create a sleep schedule

Getting a good night's sleep requires constant effort. It doesn't happen overnight (pun intended!).

What to do? Commit to a bedtime and wake-up time that allows you to get at least seven to nine hours of sleep each night. In the hours before sleep, try to reduce your exposure to blue light. I love apps that block blue light. Bright computer screens and TV screens are enemies of sleep. They'll make your body think it's daytime. Avoid caffeine and alcohol before bedtime. Finally, make your sleep environment a sanctuary. Reduce noise; adjust the temperature, and remove tempting items. (Hint: your smartphone is one of them.)

Example in practice: In 2007, Arianna Huffington was making phone calls and checking her email when she passed out at her desk, breaking her cheekbone and cutting her head. She awoke in a pool of blood with her daughter standing over her. After being diagnosed with exhaustion, Huffington changed her habits. She started to see a difference in her work style, and that's when, she says, her business began to grow. She has since become an advocate for getting enough sleep.

avoid substances and destructive behavior

Tackle any addictions or compulsive or obsessive behaviors that might be hurting your body. This includes any use abuse of nicotine, alcohol, drugs, gambling, social media, video games, pornography, work, food, or any other destructive substances and behaviors that can be hard to change. Addictions wreak havoc on the leader, but also on all those who work with that leader and those who are dependent on or love that leader. To stay healthy, consider joining one of many 12-step programs. You might also require counseling and/or medication. Seems like a lot? What's the cost of a few meetings versus irreparable damage to yourself, your career, and your loved ones? And just in case you think nobody knows, you're mistaken.

your physical stress experiments

You know the drill. Using Table 8.1 on page 167, list the physical training activities you do on a regular basis as well as one or two new physical activities you are committing to starting tomorrow or in the near future. Remember to list when you will start and when you will stop. It is always easier to commit to doing a new activity for one week than forever. Don't forget to enlist a friend for your support and accountability.

To jog your memory, here are step-by-step instructions for how to complete the stress solution worksheet:

▸ *Physical problem.* Describe the issue you are trying to solve.

▸ *What I'm doing now.* List how you've been trying to solve it.

▸ *Experimental stress solution.* Explain what new stress solution you will experiment with.

▸ *Start and end date.* List the start and end dates of your new stress solution.

▸ *Results and observations.* Write out the results of the experiment. Describe what you observed, what you learned, and any adjustments you might commit to in the future. Will you continue this stress solution?

1. Physical Problem	2. What I'm Doing Now	3. Experimental Stress Solution	4. Start and End Date	5. Results and Observations
Bone density is lacking as a current priority.	Nothing. Getting older seems far away.	Take the stairs at work and during commute. 5 pushups a day. 5 squats a day.	Saturday to Saturday (7 days)	It was hard. But got easier, and now it's a routine/habit.

TABLE 8.1 **physical stress experiment log**

chapter wrap-up

How active are you each day? What is your nutritional and supplement intake like from week to week? How common is it for you to get seven to nine hours of sleep each night? What actions can you take to alter your physical regimen to reduce stress and improve your overall health? Now that you've selected one or two stress solutions to experiment with to improve your physical finger, you've taken a major step forward in terms of enhancing your effectiveness as a leader. It's now time to move on to your last finger to wave away stress: the spiritual finger.

chapter 9

the spiritual finger

You don't need to believe in God to believe in the potential of spirituality to reduce your stress. Embracing your spirituality can help you uncover what is most meaningful in your life. It can help you find your inner self and connect with the world around you. Regardless of where you find spirituality, it can be a transformative way to reduce stress. Research shows that individuals who are more religious or spiritual are better able to cope with stress. Among the most eye-opening studies are the following:

▸ One 1998 study found the average stay among hospitalized people who never attended church was three times longer than for regular churchgoers.

▸ Another study found that heart patients were 14 times more likely to die following surgery if they did not practice a religion.

▸ Another 1992 study found that elderly people who never or rarely attended church exhibited a stroke rate double that of people who attended regularly.[1]

Spirituality, whether religious or not, has been found to promote well-being. It is associated with increased levels of happiness, a lower risk of depression and suicide, longer life expectancy, higher resiliency, and greater life satisfaction.[2] Prayer has also been associated with a host of benefits: It empowers individuals to find comfort, deal with difficult emotions, forgive others, and forge stronger, healthier relationships.

An estimated 42 percent of highly spiritual people will meditate when stressed rather than overeat or engage in unhealthy coping behaviors.[3] Meditation has been shown to increase cerebral blood flow. The focused attention that results from meditation increases the neurotransmitters responsible for establishing new neural connections. Meditation can train your brain to function differently and make better choices in certain situations.[4] It helps you focus on the present, avoid mental traps, and resist getting tangled in emotions. Take the quick quiz in Figure 9.1 on page 171 to chart your spirituality.

spirituality

As an executive, committing to spirituality can be transformative. It can help you arrive at work each day inspired by a greater sense of purpose and meaning. Consider adopting a mindfulness or meditation practice. As the Dalai Lama once said, "My true religion

Do you consider yourself to be spiritual? Respond to the following statements according to whether you believe them to be true ("T") or false ("F").

Effect	True ("T") or False ("F")
1. I believe that miracles happen.	
2. Seeing flowers bloom in the summer gives me joy.	
3. I go to church regularly.	
4. I practice meditation or mindfulness regularly.	
5. I would enjoy a silent retreat.	
6. I would like to develop a stronger sense of self.	

The more "T"s you responded with, the more likely it is that spirituality is an integral part of your life. If you don't consider yourself spiritual, keep an open mind as you read this section. Spirituality comes in many forms and flavors. There's something that resonates with everyone. Regardless of what form it takes, spirituality can significantly enhance your abilities as a leader.

FIGURE 9.1 **quiz: how spiritual are you?**

is kindness." If you are religious, consider reading scripture or attending religious services.

A lack of purpose in life can cause high stress levels. Embracing spirituality might be the key to finding that purpose. Here are some stress solutions to try.

develop meaning and connection

Developing a strong sense of meaning and connection is an important part of flexing your spiritual finger.

What to do? Always be present in conversation. When meeting with people, don't multitask. Give your friends, colleagues, family members, and others your entire attention. Listen intently, note their body gestures and facial expressions, and take time to contemplate what they are saying. Look for positives whenever possible.

Example in practice: Whenever I'm in the presence of others, I try to develop a strong sense of connection with them. I find that by shifting focus from myself to another person, it helps me establish a connection to something that is bigger than myself.

meditate

Meditation is another key way of flexing your spiritual finger. With the hectic pace of modern life, you need to take time to find peace. Carving out time to meditate can help calm your mind.

What to do? Devote at least three minutes each day to your meditation practice. Make sure you are sitting comfortably. Focus on a single point: stare at a flickering light or listen to a repetitive single sound. This strong focus will help calm and soothe the mind. Now close your eyes and let your breath rise and fall naturally. Focus on your diaphragm as you inhale and exhale.

Example in practice: I have a colleague who makes time each day to meditate. It helps her transform her negative thoughts into positive ones and find peace. Her focus remains high for hours after meditating.

find a way to worship

While worship is often associated with religion, it is much broader. Worship is an opportunity to build a stronger connection to the soul and establish a greater sense of meaning in life. For some people, it means a weekly church visit. For others, it involves a daily prayer. For still others, it is simply a time of deep thought and reflection. Regardless of the form, it's a key way to develop your spiritual finger.

What to do? Decide what form you'd like your worship to take, and commit to performing it at least three times a week for 20 minutes each time. A key part of worshiping often involves paying homage. Close your eyes, and think about something you are grateful for. Bathe your thoughts in your gratitude and appreciate the good. I've found this practice to be very helpful.

Example in practice: My neighbor had been relapsing in his drinking for years. He was a functional alcoholic, meaning that he could keep his job and look relatively passable from the outside. We often passed each other on our way to work. One day, I noticed he was walking differently and asked him what had changed. He told me he had found peace in the serenity prayer and had some slogans, too. I was interested in learning more, and before I knew it, I found myself invited to an "open" Alcoholics Anonymous meeting. I was inspired and humbled by the amount of gratitude and joy I saw as people from all walks of life held hands and said the serenity prayer. During the meeting, one man shared that he wasn't sure whether there was a "higher power," but just the idea that he could turn his life over to something other than himself helped him. In the same building, there were meetings for Al-Anon, Narcotics Anonymous, Gamblers Anonymous, Sex Addicts Anonymous, and Workaholics Anonymous—all based on a belief in a power greater than ourselves.

do some yoga

Yoga can be a valuable antidote against stress. It uses a series of postures and poses called asanas to help you achieve peace of mind and body. The combination of meditation and movement helps achieve awareness and harmony in the mind and body. Adding yoga to your daily routine can strengthen your spiritual finger.

What to do? Find a yoga class to join. Yoga studios are your best bet. If you're a beginner, it's often best to work under the guidance and support of a qualified instructor. Learning the right body postures and movements is critical to achieving harmony between the body and the soul.

Example in practice: As part of an initiative to reduce the cost of benefits and improve employee health, one of my clients created a wellness program that involved eating, moving, and yoga. I didn't go to their offices for a few months, and when I came back I noticed the difference to the point that I planned some of my project meetings right after "lunch yoga" because people were receptive, collaborative, and at peace. They even sat up straight! I personally enjoy some light yoga after working out. Combined with reflection and gratitude, it just makes everything right.

spend time in nature

Spending time making friends with all things green can do wonders for your stress levels. "Forest-bathing" can be a transformative experience. Your ability to conquer stress will boost to new heights if you make time for nature in your life.

What to do? Commit to fully immersing yourself in nature for at least 30 minutes a day. Walk to work; take a stroll in the park, or book a weekend hiking trip. It's up to you. Being around nature increases your blood flow and puts your body into a state of calm. When in nature, listen intently to the sounds. Let them relax you and ease your mind. Breathe deeply in the rich oxygen that surrounds you.

Example in practice: Did you know that there are bison in the city of San Francisco? San Francisco has many parks that are well-cared for by the community, and I find great joy in running and walking the city trails. I stop to marvel at the turtles, the birds, the bison, and the ocean at the end of Golden Gate Park. I love the taste of the air as the fog rolls in every day. Taking time to enjoy nature is a gift. It's good to be alive, really alive.

your spiritual stress experiments

Using Table 9.1 on page 175, list the spiritual training activities you do on a regular basis as well as one or two new spiritual activities you are committing to starting tomorrow or in the near future. Remember to list when you will start and when you will stop. It is always easier to commit to doing a new activity for one week than forever. Don't forget to enlist a friend for support and accountability.

To jog your memory, here are step-by-step instructions for how to complete the stress solution worksheet below:

▸ *Spiritual problem.* Describe the issue you are trying to solve.

▸ *What I'm doing now.* List how you've been trying to solve it.

▸ *Experimental stress solution.* Explain what new stress solution you will experiment with.

▸ *Start and end date.* List the start and end dates of your new stress solution.

▸ *Results and observations.* Write out the results of the experiment. Describe what you observed, what you learned, and any adjustments you might make in the future. Will you continue this stress solution?

1. Spiritual Problem	2. What I'm Doing Now	3. Experimental Stress Solution	4. Start and End Date	5. Results and Observations

TABLE 9.1 **spiritual stress experiment log**

chapter wrap-up

Do you feel a strong sense of purpose in life? Do you feel like you are part of a bigger picture? When making decisions, do you think about the implications for your community and the world? In this chapter, you selected one or two stress solutions to experiment with to improve your spiritual finger. In the coming days, reflect on what you learn and how much benefit you reap from each experiment.

Enhancing your spiritual capabilities is an important, although often overlooked, component of leadership.

Now that you've learned what you can do as a leader to tackle your own stress levels, it's time to shift to looking at what role companies play. In Chapter 10, you'll learn about the many steps companies can take to help tackle and prevent stress. Early treatment is one of the keys to dealing with stress in the workplace. Whatever the cause, it's much easier to deal with stress in its early stages.

a call for action beyond you and me

ost people can agree that companies have a responsibility to reduce stress in the workplace. Robert
Blendon, a professor at the Harvard T.H. Chan
School of Public Health, has gone so far as to say, "Job number one for U.S. employers is to reduce stress in the workplace."[1] Blendon was one of the principal researchers in a
2016 study focused on health in the workplace, which found

that 44 percent of working adults report that their job has a negative impact on their stress levels. You are certainly not alone.

Quoted in *The Harvard Gazette*, Blendon stated, "Many . . . health problems can be corrected if companies adopt a much more significant role in creating a 'culture of health' in the workplace where workers feel empowered to pursue living a healthier life."[2] He clearly sees stress reduction as part of a broader attempt to improve health and well-being in the workplace. But is such an attempt even possible?

The evidence suggests yes, but it requires careful planning and implementation. A 2017 study by the University of California Riverside found that companies that offered employee wellness programs saw a significant gain in worker productivity. The researchers determined that those workers who took advantage of the program boosted their productivity levels by one full workday per month on average.

Do you think your role or occupation has an especially high level of stress? Stress is a universal phenomenon, but different occupations and industries report different levels of stress. Some of the most common sources of stress include a lack of job security, unrealistic job expectations, low salaries, tight deadlines, toxic co-workers, and minimal opportunity for growth and advancement.

Unsurprisingly, many of these stressors affect leaders as well. Consider unrealistic job expectations, which often occur when there is a lack of resources. Perhaps it's not enough time or not enough training. Many of these stressors affect every level of a company, whether the result is layoffs, increased workloads, or fear of losing their jobs.

In this chapter, you'll learn how companies can take proactive and reactive steps toward addressing their employees' stress. While companies have a moral obligation to reduce stress, it's also in their best interest to keep stress levels at bay. Doing so will increase employee engagement, enhance recruiting efforts, and improve the bottom line. First, let's use the quiz in Figure 10.1 on page 179 to assess your workplace stress.

Now it's time to assess your own workplace stress. The following table includes a list of common job stressors. Beside each one, on a scale of 1 to 5 (with "1" indicating hardly at all and "5" indicating a significant effect), rate each stressor according to how much it affects you in your current role. In the right-hand column, think about one small or large action that you'd be willing to take to confront the stressor head-on.

Stressor	Rating (1-5)	Action Item
Tight deadlines		
Long commute		
Work-life balance		
Heavy workload		
Toxic co-workers		
Lack of advancement opportunities		
Difficult targets		
Lack of resources		

Take note of the stressors you rated "4" or "5." The first step toward reducing stress and preventing it from derailing your effectiveness is to understand which stresses you are most vulnerable to.

FIGURE 10.1 **quiz: assessing your workplace stress**

a culture of stress

Each year, CareerCast.com releases a report on the most stressful U.S. jobs.[3] It takes into account career growth potential, physical demands, environmental conditions, competition, risk of death or grievous injury, deadlines, and working in the public eye. If you had to guess, what is the most stressful job revealed by CareerCast's 2018 report?

Did you guess firefighter? Or pilot? Maybe police officer? These are all high on the list, but none of them holds the top spot. Enlisted military personnel ranked first.

The other occupations on CareerCast's top list, in order of descending stress levels, include:

1. Firefighter
2. Airline Pilot
3. Police Officer
4. Event Coordinator
5. Newspaper Reporter
6. Broadcaster
7. Public Relations Executive
8. Senior Corporate Executive
9. Taxi Driver

Looking at the list, it isn't hard to understand why these occupations drive high stress levels. Like enlisted military personnel, risking their lives on the job is a real possibility for firefighters and police officers. Airline pilots travel long distances and spend a lot of time away from family and friends. Event coordinators, newspaper reporters, and senior corporate executives are always up against strict deadlines, while PR executives and broadcasters constantly face public scrutiny.

High stress levels among workers are alarming, so it's not surprising that many organizations have taken action to correct them. "Buddy systems" encourage police officers to support each other. Generous retirement benefits have been offered to public service workers, and counseling services are available for many employees.

But it's not enough. Stress carries a hefty price tag for all companies. Two-thirds of Americans say that work is a primary source of stress in their lives, and approximately 30 percent of workers report "extreme stress levels."[4]

the cost of stress

Have you ever missed a day of work due to stress? If so, you're not alone. According to a whitepaper produced by Health Advocate, the leading independent and healthcare advocacy and assistance company in the U.S., the costs associated with workplace stress are far-reaching and include:[5]

> ▸ *Disability, accidents, and workers' comp claims.* Stress-related distraction or sleepiness is responsible for approximately 60 to 80 percent of accidents on the job.
>
> ▸ *Absenteeism.* It's estimated that 1 million employees miss work each day due to stress. Absenteeism is responsible for 26 percent of health-related lost productivity in the workplace.
>
> ▸ *Presenteeism.* The opposite of absenteeism, presenteeism happens when employees come to work but cannot perform up to their full potential. Sixty percent of workers report losing productivity due to stress. Costs associated with presenteeism total $150 billion each year, according to the International Foundation of Employee Benefit Plans.
>
> ▸ *Physical effects.* Stressed workers' health-care costs are 46 percent higher than non-stressed employees'. Some 60 to 90 percent of doctor visits can be attributed to stress-related illnesses and symptoms.
>
> ▸ *Psychological effects.* Stressed workers face increased risk of mental health problems and are more susceptible to short tempers. It's estimated that depression alone has resulted in $31 billion a year in lost workdays.

You can rank your workplace stresses in the personal challenge assessment in Figure 10.2 on page 182.

As you can imagine, the costs associated with workplace accidents, absenteeism, turnover, diminished productivity, medical and insurance costs, and workers' comp awards add up fast. According to The American Institute of Stress, the annual cost of work-related stress in the U.S. is $300 billion.[6] To put that into perspective, it's almost one-third of the U.S. federal budget deficit.

It seems like a no-brainer: Minimize stress in the workplace, and you'll increase productivity and decrease absenteeism and

Now that we've learned about the costs associated with workplace stress, rank each one on a scale of 1 to 5 (with "1" indicating no effect and "5" indicating a significant effect), according to how much each affects your company.

Cost	Severity (1–5)
Disability, accidents, and workers' comp claims	
Absenteeism	
Presenteeism	
Physical effects	
Psychological effects	

FIGURE 10.2 **personal challenge: workplace stresses**

attrition. Performance will spike and health costs will plummet. It's a win-win-win.

how companies address stress

Companies seem to recognize the importance of reducing stress. Many dedicate a large portion of their budgets to health and wellness policies and initiatives. In recent years, General Motors has reportedly spent more on health care than on steel.

Companies offer many different programs that target stress. You need to consider what programs you can implement, depending on the size or scale of your business. If you're an entrepreneur, solopreneur, or small business, you'll likely need to make some tough decisions about what benefits you can afford to offer. Reflect on your stress reduction efforts in Figure 10.3 on page 183.

employee assistance programs

Employee assistance programs (EAPs) are employer-sponsored programs designed to alleviate stress and other workplace-related issues. They may offer services such as career planning, financial

While you may think your organization doesn't do enough to address stress, chances are it is doing something. Perhaps it offers health-care benefits or counseling. Using the table below, write down everything your company does to help reduce stress. Then, on a scale of 1 to 5 (with "1" indicating not at all effective and "5" indicating extremely effective, rate each one according to how effective it is at reducing stress.

Stress Reduction Effort	Effectiveness (1–5)

FIGURE 10.3 **personal reflection: stress reduction efforts**

advice, and legal advice. They may also offer support for weight loss, smoking cessation, mental health, and addiction. EAPs are very common among larger companies: More than 97 percent of large companies in the U.S. (defined as companies with more than 5,000 employees) offer confidential EAPs.[7] The top reason employees access EAP services is stress. Surprise, surprise! Other reasons include relationship concerns, child behavior, anxiety, depression, occupational issues, and legal issues.[8]

EAPs can do a lot of good. They can reduce stress, depression, and absenteeism. They've even been linked to increased psychosocial functioning[9] and enhanced work relationships.[10] And the company gets a lot of bang for its buck: EAPs produce a $3 to $10 return for every dollar invested.[11]

Given that EAPs are so common and offer so many benefits, it's curious that so few employees actually take advantage of them: A mere 7 percent of employees in North America use their EAPs.[12] Why is this? In some cases, it's simply because employees aren't aware that their company offers an EAP. In other cases, employees are apprehensive that the services are really confidential.

As you roll out your EAP (if your company doesn't already have one), it's critical to choose the right communication strategy. If your EAP is difficult to navigate or improperly communicated, adoption rates will be dismal. It's like throwing money in the garbage. To ensure the EAP's success, focus on building strong communication channels and provide a confidential, anonymous way for employees to review the program. You can set up a corporate FAQ to outline the features and benefits of the EAP. You can organize town halls to brief employees on the EAP's features and administer surveys every quarter to measure engagement levels and identify opportunities for improvement. If you're an entrepreneur and can't afford a comprehensive EAP, there are lots of similar cost-effective alternatives. You can hire counselors or provide links to helpful online resources and counseling services. Keep track of your company's EAP offerings in the personal challenge in Figure 10.4 below.

Do you know whether your organization offers an EAP? Chances are high it does. Research your company's EAP and use the following table to record all the services it offers.

Service Offered	Have I Used/Will I Use This Service?

FIGURE 10.4 **personal challenge: your company's eap**

wellness programs and benefits

In addition to (or as part of) an EAP, you can offer wellness programs and benefits. These may include fitness program reimbursements, on-site gyms, weight-loss programs, smoking cessation programs, health screenings, vaccination clinics, transportation reimbursements, and mindfulness training. For example, a yoga class can be implemented even at the smallest startups. As with EAPs, your company can benefit financially by implementing wellness programs. One study found that stock appreciation among the 45 companies with best-in-breed wellness programs was 235 percent from 2009 to 2014, as compared to 159 percent for the S&P 500 during the same five-year period.[13] That shouldn't be dismissed lightly.

Just like EAPs, strong communication and awareness of wellness programs is critical. Time and again, I've seen that responsibility fall on HR. Unfortunately, HR rarely has a budget for internal communications. EAPs and wellness programs can quickly become companies' best-kept secrets. Unsurprisingly, companies that cite a positive ROI associated with wellness programs are more likely to have established strong communication channels than companies that do not.[14]

How familiar are you with your company's EAP and wellness programs? Does it offer some type of mindfulness program? Mindfulness training in the workplace has gained a lot of traction in recent years. A 2016 study by the National Business Group on Health (NBGH) and Fidelity Investments found that 22 percent of companies have implemented mindfulness training programs.[15] At Aetna, employees who participated in mindfulness training offered by the insurance company realized an average of 62 minutes of increased productivity each week, which saved the company $3,000 per employee each year.[16] Many companies have started to offer their employees subscriptions or subsidies to smartphone apps such as Calm, Headspace, and Muse. Do you have a mindfulness app on your phone? Why not give it a try? There are many free apps available.

pto policies

When was the last time you took a vacation? A healthy paid time off (PTO) policy goes a long way toward reducing stress levels. If you're a solopreneur and can't take PTO, it's still important to pencil vacation time into your schedule. Many companies in the U.S. have started implementing unlimited vacation policies, which sounds too good to be true. It actually might be—these policies are less effective than initially thought. Research has found that companies that offer unlimited vacation time actually encourage employees to take less time off.[17] Talk about irony! It appears employees have internalized stress so vigorously that the thought of taking additional time off increases their stress levels.

Workers are taking fewer vacation days than they have in years. In 1996, the average number of vacation days used by each worker was 21. By 2016, it had plummeted to 16. Workers have lost almost an entire week of vacation time in just 20 years![18] The United States is the only country in the Organisation for Economic Co-operation and Development (OECD) that does not mandate paid vacation for workers. The European Union guarantees its workers at least 20 paid vacation days per year. Many European countries, including the United Kingdom, France, Austria, Denmark, Finland, Luxembourg, and Sweden, require 25 or more paid vacation days each year.

Company culture has a large impact on motivating or demotivating employees to schedule vacation time, as does manager influence. As a leader, you should build a business case for vacation time. Research indicates that if you use 11 or more of your vacation days, you are more than 30 percent *more* likely to receive a raise.[19] This should be a wake-up call to you and your employees—why not schedule your next vacation right now?

The onus should be on you as a leader to reiterate the business case for vacations to your workers. You must encourage them to take vacation time, and you must manage their expectations and reduce their workloads to enable their time off. If employees fear they'll return to a Mount Everest pile of work on their desk, they'll never leave. One study found that employees who were concerned they would be perceived as less dedicated or even replaceable for taking a vacation were significantly less likely to take advantage of their vacation time.[20] You need to set a positive example by taking ample vacation time yourself. Healthy expectations around vacation time are especially important for solopreneurs and entrepreneurs, who are often time- and resource-strapped. The time away from the office can help you gain a new perspective and return to your work rejuvenated.

Use the personal challenge in Figure 10.5 below to reflect on your vacation time (or the lack thereof).

Are you in need of a vacation? If I had to guess, I'd say you're probably long overdue. Most people wouldn't keep postponing or even forgo doctors' appointments, paying rent, or renewing their driver's licenses. So why are vacations different? What's holding you back? Using the following table, indicate whether any of the statements are affecting your decision to take a vacation using "Y" for "Yes" or "N" for "No". For those that are, write down an action item for how to address them.

Reason to Postpone/ Forgo Vacation	Effect on Vacation Decision? ("Y"/"N")	Action Item
I'm afraid I'll come back to a huge workload.		
I'm afraid it will make me look bad.		
I'm afraid I will lose money.		
I'm afraid my co-workers will need me.		
I don't know where to go.		

The more "Y"s you responded with, the more likely you're in need of a vacation.

FIGURE 10.5 **personal challenge: vacation time?**

office design

How often do you think about your office environment? Do you work in an office with an open-plan layout? If so, do you find yourself constantly distracted by your co-workers?

Open-plan office layouts have been around for more than a century, but they exploded as a trend in the early 2000s, embraced by tech companies like Apple and Facebook. While there are many cost benefits associated with open offices, there are several indirect costs that are often swept under the carpet. For one thing, open-plan office layouts can be noisy. According to one study, almost 60 percent of workers reported that noise such as conversations, amplified by the open-office layout, caused distraction and stress.[21] Another study showed that even low-level office noise can increase stress hormone levels.[22] Open-office layouts typically have noise levels in the range of 60 to 65 decibels. To put this in perspective, the hum of a refrigerator is in the range of 40 decibels, and a busy highway is approximately 85 decibels. How noisy is your office?

Make efforts to reconfigure your workplace to minimize environmentally induced stress. Natural lighting, plants and other green elements, improved airflow, and quiet rooms can all help reduce stress. Research indicates that by lowering noise levels with sound-absorbing ceilings, furniture, and/or white noise machines, employee focus increases 48 percent.[23]

tackling stress with organizational development interventions

While some stress can be addressed through policies at the organizational level, much of it is associated with business practices and must be dealt with by leaders. It is incumbent on you as a leader to meet with colleagues and discuss how to promote healthier stress levels. Strategic planning should be top-of-mind. Ongoing strategic planning helps the company respond to changing market dynamics and avoid the whiplash that can result when unnecessary changes are made. Strategic planning should be followed by careful budgeting. Involvement and buy-in from all leaders is critical.

Companies should leverage a number of different organizational development interventions in their efforts to tackle stress. In addition to the EAPs you've already read about, here are some more initiatives companies can implement to reduce stress.

strategic planning

Strategic planning helps companies remain agile and responsive to customer demands while allowing you to avoid undue harm caused by unpredictable changes. In doing so, it reduces stress. Strategic planning also helps the executive team understand and agree on their company's core mission, values, and objectives. Buy-in from all members of the executive team is critical. Think about your last strategic-planning initiative: Was it successful? What changes would you make?

budget planning

Do you know how budget planning really happens at your company? Is funding secured by a vote? Does someone have a final say? Budget planning should happen after strategic planning. It should also take place once a year as a collaborative effort. If you're an entrepreneur or solopreneur, try to enlist outside experts when finalizing your budget. If you work at a larger company, all senior leaders should be involved. Individual leaders should be given the freedom to define their budgets, but the process shouldn't be self-serving—each project should be clearly outlined and vetted.

position control

Position control is a process that involves creating, maintaining, and monitoring positions and their budgets. If you're a solopreneur or entrepreneur, your company may not be mature enough to benefit from position control. But if you work at a larger company, there are innumerable benefits.

The process is quite simple in theory. All members of the executive team typically receive control of head count, titles, and salaries for their teams. Any additional requests require a business case for action that should be reviewed by the executive team. Position control helps prevent jockeying over resources and limits the politics that are often involved in establishing head count. The result is reduced stress (and fewer sleepless nights). Sound appealing? If you haven't considered position control, it's time to give it careful thought.

talent review

Talent reviews help you understand your talent pools and should be conducted once a year (are you seeing a theme?). If you're a solopreneur or entrepreneur, you will spearhead the effort, with input from any cofounders and senior employees. If you work at a larger company, the talent review process should involve all members of the executive team. Each executive should carefully review their direct reports and outline their strengths and areas for development. Team members are usually assessed on a 3-by-3 matrix, like the one in Figure 10.6 on page 191, that evaluates employees on two dimensions: past performance and future potential. Performance is typically measured on the horizontal axis and potential is measured on the vertical axis. This process ensures consistency in evaluation and prevents overemphasizing current performance. When was the last time you participated in a talent review? If it's been a year or longer, you're falling short in terms of helping your employees reach their full potential.

succession planning

When was the last time one of your co-workers, employees, or direct reports resigned unexpectedly? It's more common than you might think. Succession planning is essential for business continuity. It helps your company remain fluid and dynamic and prevents abrupt gaps in positions caused by resignation, termination, ill-health, and retirement. As a best practice, you as a leader, along with the rest of the executive team, should identify at least one potential successor for each key employee. You should also evaluate each successor's readiness for the role and outline recommended development opportunities. This process ensures seamless and successful transitions and avoids a stressed workforce and unnecessarily high human capital costs.

leadership development

Your company's success depends on its ability to develop its leaders. You should create an individual development plan (IDP), or a plan for moving forward in the company and in their career, for each employee. Focus especially on employees located in the upper right-hand corner of the 3-by-3 matrix we discussed earlier. Monitor IDPs on a quarterly basis and reevaluate as employees develop skills, gain competencies, and transition to new positions. Research shows that

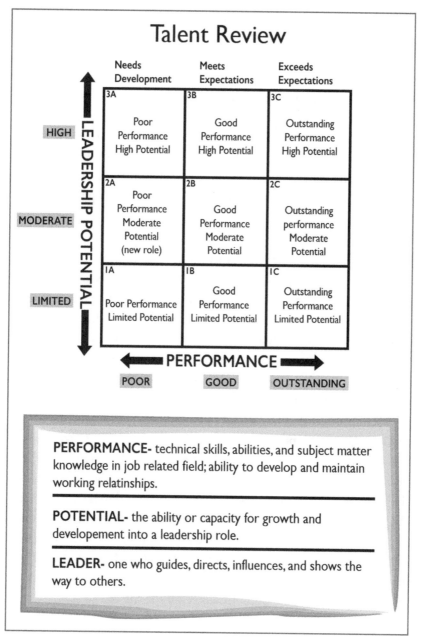

FIGURE 10.6 **3-by-3 talent review matrix**

organizations that make strong commitments to talent development perform better in the marketplace.

Executive coaches are transformative in developing key leaders. They can help create IDPs, and they also help aspiring leaders develop crucial skills, including self-awareness, empathy, influence, executive communication, visionary leadership, strategic thinking, and ambiguity management. Sure, there are many online resources aimed at leadership development. But these are most effective at helping leaders develop *technical* skills. Executive coaching offers a dynamic, interactive, and highly engaging environment where leaders can engage in deep reflection, change their mindsets, develop their emotional intelligence, and increase their leadership capabilities.

board roles and relations

Your company's board of directors is essential to ensuring its prosperity. Typically, a company's board is comprised of at least three committees: an executive committee, a governance committee, and a finance committee. The executive committee helps establish strategic goals and evaluate the performance of the company and CEO; the governance committee is responsible for managing the board and recruiting new members; and the finance committee oversees the company's budget and the financing process.

It's important that the relationships among your board members, as well as the one between the board and your CEO, are strong. Board members have a responsibility to advocate for and advance the business and to act honestly and in the best interests of the company. They also need to understand their fiduciary duties, respect the CEO's interests, and avoid micromanaging. Board members should never give directions to the CEO's direct reports. Boards have been sued and held personally accountable for ethical oversights. They must act as the public face of the company and develop outside relationships that allow them to advocate for the business.

strong communication channels

Effective communication is critical to managing stress. Strong, constant communication ensures a cohesive environment and boosts morale. When employees understand their company's direction, they feel more secure. As a leader, you're responsible for creating this safe environment. Not only does it reduce stress, but it also improves work ethic—everyone begins working together toward a common goal. Company town halls can help ensure that employees are kept informed, engaged, and inspired. Office hours can also reinforce strong communication. By giving employees access to senior leadership, your company can demonstrate that it is committed to ensuring employees have the required resources to develop their abilities and reach their potential.

The costs associated with workplace stress, including workers' comp claims, absenteeism, presenteeism, and psychological effects, are immense. Your company has a responsibility to foster an environment that targets stress from many angles. EAPs, wellness programs, lenient time-off policies, and effective office design can all do wonders for creating a workplace that minimizes stress and empowers organizations to succeed. Even solopreneurs and entrepreneurs can implement small-scale platforms that target stress and increase well-being.

chapter wrap-up

Thus far, you've learned about an arsenal of tools and tactics you can draw upon to quell your stress levels and the stress levels at your company. For the most part, these have been reactive coping techniques. They are highly effective, but they are only the bare-bones foundation for tackling stress. In the remainder of the book, we'll focus on you as a leader and spotlight more proactive ways to deal with stress. In Chapter 11, you'll learn to heal from stress. In Chapter 12, you'll learn how to prevent it. Finally, in Chapter 13, you'll learn how to develop resiliency against stress and enhance your longevity. You'll be empowered for a life of stress-less leadership.

your path to recovery

S tress is like a wound: Healing from it involves a period of recovery. But unlike healing from an injury, curing stress is not a natural restorative response. Effective recovery requires conscious effort, forgiveness, and support. In this chapter, we'll discuss why forgiveness and support are such a critical part of the healing process. By understanding their impact on stress, you'll gain the strength to embark on a successful recovery process and prevent future stress. Forgiveness is rarely discussed in the context of leadership, but leaders who forgive themselves and others gain tremendous respect and trust from others. Just like many other leadership skills, forgiveness is a muscle that can be built and strengthened over time.

forgiveness

Forgiveness is a conscious and deliberate decision to pardon someone who has harmed or adversely affected you. It does not mean forgetting, condoning, or excusing offenses. It's about liberating yourself from anger and negative feelings and achieving peace of mind.

Stress is often caused by the actions of others. A customer demands a full refund for a purchase without a valid explanation. A co-worker reneges on a commitment to help with a project. Your boss tells you at the last minute that you will have to work all weekend to complete a business proposal. Afterward, you feel bitter. You hold a grudge. It's difficult to let go of these feelings, and your stress levels go into overdrive as a result. One study found that when people held on to a grudge, they experienced heightened physiological activity, including muscle tension, increased heart rate, higher blood pressure, and even sweating, compared to when they forgave.[1] Charlotte vanOyen-Witvliet, the lead researcher for the study, explained, "When people think about their offenders in unforgiving ways, they tend to experience stronger negative emotions and greater stress responses. In contrast, when these same people think about their offenders in more forgiving ways, they tend to experience great positive emotion, greater perceived control, and less potent negative emotion and stress in the short term."[2]

How often do you forgive others? Forgiveness is not for the faint of heart. It's difficult and unnatural. It's important to note that forgiveness does not mean you would allow the person to cross you again. A frequently quoted Gallup poll found that 94 percent of people said it's important to forgive, but only 48 percent said they usually attempted to forgive others.[3] When people do decide to forgive, many practice conditional forgiveness, pledging to forgive only if the offender apologizes or promises not to commit the offense again. A 2011 study published in the *Journal of Behavioral Medicine* found that people who practice conditional forgiveness may be more likely to die earlier than those who are less likely to engage in the practice.[4] Take the quiz in Figure 11.1 to see how forgiving you are.

How forgiving are you? Answer the following statements according to whether they are true ("T") or false ("F").

Statement	True ("T") or False ("F")
When someone upsets me, I tend to keep as much distance as possible.	
When someone hurts me, I want to see them pay.	
When an otherwise reliable colleague lets me down, I'm unlikely to forgive him quickly.	
I've held a grudge against someone for more than a year.	

The more statements you answered with "T," the less naturally forgiveness comes to you. This chapter will help you reconceptualize forgiveness and reframe your natural tendencies.

FIGURE 11.1 **quiz: forgiveness**

Leaders often find forgiveness difficult, viewing it as a sign of weakness or frailty. But forgiveness is essential to stress recovery and prevention. It can offset some of the long-term effects of chronic stress. One study found that when individuals are highly forgiving of both themselves and others, it virtually eliminated the link between stress and mental illness.[5] The study's author, Loren Toussaint, explained, "If you don't have forgiving tendencies, you feel the raw effects of stress in an unmitigated way. You don't have a buffer against that stress."

When was the last time you forgave someone? Sixty-two percent of Americans say they need more forgiveness in their personal lives, according to a survey by the Fetzer Institute.[6] It's not difficult to understand why. According to the Mayo Clinic, there are so many benefits associated with forgiveness, including lower stress levels, improved mental health, lower levels of anxiety and hostility, lower blood pressure, fewer symptoms of depression, a stronger immune system, improved heart health, and higher self-esteem.[7]

Do you wish you were better at forgiving? An important first step is to show empathy toward your offender. This involves shifting your perspective. You can also improve your ability to forgive by managing your emotions. Research has shown that your ability to manage and repair your emotions makes you more likely to forgive.[8]

making amends

While forgiveness often involves others, forgiving yourself is essential to the stress healing process. Everyone makes rash decisions and judgments that they later regret. When you ruminate about your actions, it only causes more stress. Reflect on your strained relationships. Think carefully about any harm you've inflicted. Admit your own mistakes. And then express a genuine desire to improve the relationship. Making amends helps you forgive the offender, including yourself. A study published in *The Journal of Positive Psychology* found that individuals who asked for forgiveness for a wrongdoing were more likely to also forgive themselves.[9] A key to forgiving yourself is giving yourself permission to let go. Don't assume that you deserve to feel badly. Use the personal challenge chart in Figure 11.2 on page 199 to think about how you have made amends.

social support

Social support is a critical part of the stress recovery process. The healing process is much more effective when you have strong connections you can rely on. This support can come in many forms. People who have a close network of friends or colleagues are better at tackling stress. Companies that encourage co-worker bonding are more likely to have peer support networks.

Reflect on your relationship with one person you've hurt in some way. Have they also hurt you? Was your relationship strong in the past? What was the inflection point? Record this in the first column of the table below. Next talk to the person, own up to your mistake, and tell them you'd like to repair the relationship. Record your experience in the second column. Now determine the best course of action. How will you forgive yourself? How will you repair the relationship? Use the final column to record the results of your journey to make amends.

Person I've Hurt	Reflections on Relationship	Reflections on Conversation	How Will I Forgive Myself?	How Will I Repair the Relationship?	Results	How Will I Make Amends?

FIGURE 11.2 **personal challenge: making amends**

Your friends and community should be your go-to place for social support. They are readily available, don't charge you for your time, and can typically relate well to your situation. Consider the friends you see every day, members of your community, old high school or college friends, members of your gym, and people who attend your place of worship. Recovery from stress can be a difficult journey, with highs and lows. Lean on your support network during the highs and even more strongly during the lows.

Executive coaches can also provide a form of social support. Coaching provides a safe environment for employees to share their fears and anxieties. One study found that coaching reduced worker stress levels even when stress was not specifically targeted.[10] Coaching also supports employees in developing effective tactics to combat stress. Another study found that workers reported they felt better equipped to cope with any future feelings of burnout as a result of coaching.[11] In addition to executive coaches, mentors can offer additional social support. Formal and informal mentors can both be beneficial to workers. While formal mentors are more likely to provide career advice, informal mentors are more likely to provide social support. Use the form in Figure 11.3 below to reflect on your mentors.

Do you have formal mentors? What about informal ones? What expertise do they bring to the table? How often do you communicate with them? Is that enough?

Mentor	Informal or Formal	Impact on Me

FIGURE 11.3 **quiz: mentors**

Research clearly indicates that forgiveness, making amends, and social support greatly alleviate stress. Contrary to belief, forgiveness need not be aimed at others. Forgiving yourself and making amends can be a potent form of stress relief, too. Social support is also a key way to prevent burnout, even if this means forging new relationships.

chapter wrap-up

Are you carrying around baggage that is decades-old? Are you carrying around guilt? Do you need to make amends? With whom? What does your social support system look like? At what point should you expand or build a new community? I hope this chapter has compelled you to take action. By forgiving others, making amends, and ensuring you have a strong social support network in place, you'll enhance your abilities and reduce your stress levels.

Up to this point, this book has focused on more reactive measures against stress, but ideally you want to prevent stress before it rears its ugly head. In Chapter 12, I'll walk you through some preventive measures you can take to protect yourself from stresses before they start.

your iron fortress against stress

oo many people wait until stress has progressed too far before taking action. Unlike other afflictions, like alcohol abuse or cancer, that only affect certain individuals, stress is ubiquitous. It affects all of us. It's inescapable. So it makes sense to take preventive measures against stress. Stress is not an "if" but a "when."

Your best chances of succeeding are to aim for prevention. In this chapter, you will discover a number of ingenious methods you can use to prevent stress on the individual and organizational level. You should select the ones that feel right to you.

time management

As an executive, you know there are never enough hours in the day. From streams of emails to floods of meeting requests, your time is under constant attack. Time management becomes more difficult as workloads increase, but it is crucial to effective leadership and stress prevention. The first step toward understanding how effective you are at time management is to do a time audit assessing how much time you spend on the activities that consume your day. To-do lists, calendar apps, and time-tracking software can all help you remain on task and better understand how effectively you are dividing your time. Use the quiz in Figure 12.1 below to assess your time management skills.

Are you good at managing your time? Using the following table, respond to the statements according to whether they are true ("T") or false ("F").

Statement	True ("T") or False ("F")
I work on the highest-priority tasks first.	
I rarely ask for extensions.	
I don't like to put off important work.	
I have a good sense for how long it will take to complete a task.	
I pencil in time for dealing with things that come up unexpectedly.	
I create to-do lists and generally complete them.	

The more "T's" you responded with, the more effective you are at time management. Regardless of how you fared, there is a lot you can do to better manage your time.

FIGURE 12.1 **quiz: time management**

procrastination prevention

English writer Edward Young called procrastination the thief of time. Procrastination is a self-handicapping behavior that prevents you from meeting deadlines and reaching peak levels of productivity. It's one of the most common workplace stressors. Procrastinators have higher levels of stress and lower well-being than those who get their work done on time.

Are you a chronic procrastinator? Ineffective time management often goes hand in hand with procrastination. However, just because you have poor time management skills doesn't mean you're a procrastinator. Although procrastination can be caused by poor time management, there are often deeper, more pressing issues at play.

While time-management training can go a long way toward preventing procrastination and the stress that comes with it, the most effective prevention mechanisms are often found at the organizational level. Procrastination is often triggered by a sense of paralysis due to a lack of role clarity.

delegating

Managers frequently struggle with delegating. Do you enjoy delegating, or does it give you anxiety? According to research, there are two psychological processes that make people more hesitant to delegate work.[1] The first is the "self-enhancement effect," which happens when a person evaluates a project or task more favorably when they are more involved in it. The second is the "faith in supervision effect," which is when a person believes that work performed under the guidance of a manager is higher quality than work performed without supervision.

Reflecting on yourself and the feedback you have received, do you consider yourself an effective delegator? Effective delegating doesn't just prevent stress and burnout among leaders, but also enhances team capacity. When leaders delegate work thoughtfully, they empower their team members to take on new responsibilities and expand their skill sets. Effective delegation involves five key steps:

1. *Evaluate.* Managers must first determine whether a task should be delegated. If it is critical for long-term success and mission-critical to the company, they may not want to delegate it. Managers must also evaluate whether they have enough time to effectively delegate the job. Delegating should not be a rapid-fire handoff. They will need to spend time training, checking on progress, and engaging in constant communication.

2. *Prepare.* Managers must map out exactly what's required. They should include clear and comprehensive information about timing, budget, milestones, communication frequency, and resources.

3. *Assign.* Managers must determine which team members have the required skill set or expertise to complete the task. Ideally, it should help employees grow and expand their capabilities.

4. *Confirm understanding and commitment.* Managers often make false assumptions about whether employees understand what is being asked of them. They should confirm understanding by asking their employees to summarize the request and what's required. Managers must also get explicit commitment from their employees, who must commit to the expected results, milestones, resource requirements, and proposed budget.

5. *Avoid micromanaging.* Once managers hand off the baton, it's critical to avoid micromanaging. If an employee hits a roadblock, managers should treat this as a learning opportunity, not take the reins. Effective coaching will help employees understand where they've gone wrong and help empower them to succeed in the future.

Use the personal challenge in Figure 12.2 on page 207 to see how effectively you delegate tasks.

Delegating tends to be particularly difficult for inexperienced managers. If you struggle with delegation, consider blocking off time each day to create a plan of action. With careful planning, you and your team can succeed. Once you start delegating

Choose one task or project you might be able to delegate to one of your reports or team members. Complete the following table to determine whether it's the right type of activity to delegate and how effectively you are delegating.

Delegation Stage	Question	Response
Evaluate	Is this task critical to my long-term success?	
Evaluate	Do I have enough time to effectively delegate?	
Prepare	Have I mapped out what's required to complete the task?	
Assign	Have I determined which team member to delegate the task to?	
Assign	Does the selected individual have the required skill set?	
Confirm understanding and commitment	Have I confirmed understanding?	
Confirm understanding and commitment	Have I confirmed commitment?	
Avoid micromanaging	How will I clear the way?	
Avoid micromanaging	How will I step in if the task veers off-course?	

FIGURE 12.2 **personal challenge: delegation**

effectively, your team will dare to come forward more often and more vigorously.

avoiding overcommitment

Do you find yourself biting off more than you can chew? Overcommitment is common among executives and leaders. A strong desire to please causes workers to agree to take on tasks without considering whether they have enough bandwidth. As requests and tasks pile up on each other and deadlines draw near, employees become overwhelmed and stressed. Unsurprisingly, research has shown that overcommitment increases burnout over time.[2]

Overcommitment can be crippling and lead to a kind of paralysis. Employees either find themselves reneging on their commitments or letting the quality of their work suffer, which both incite even higher levels of stress.

In the workplace, women are especially likely to overcommit, particularly when it comes to non-promotable tasks. These are tasks that benefit the organization but aren't generally considered in career advancement or performance evaluations. These include office "housework" like organizing a team bonding event, going on a coffee run, or filling in for a coworker. One study revealed that women were 48 percent more likely to volunteer than men for a project during a work meeting.[3] Are you the go-to person for planning the company holiday party? As a leader, you should be on the lookout for which of your colleagues assume the bulk of office housework.

The most effective antidote against overcommitment is to be firm and set boundaries. You must be vigilant about protecting your time and learn how to say "no." Research indicates that there's an art and a science to saying "no." In a groundbreaking 2011 study, researchers at Boston College and the University of Houston evaluated students who had set a healthy eating goal. First the students were presented with a tempting snack and instructed to respond by saying either "I don't" or "I can't" ("I don't eat candy" vs. "I can't eat candy," for example). Next they were asked to choose between a chocolate bar and a healthy granola bar. Sixty-four percent of participants who were instructed to say "I don't" opted for the healthier granola bar, while only 39 percent of participants who were told to say "I can't" chose the healthier option.[4]

Heidi Grant, the associate director of Columbia University's Motivation Science Center, explained that the word "don't" makes all the difference: "'I don't' is experienced as a choice, so it feels empowering," she said. "It's an affirmation of your determination and willpower. 'I can't' isn't a choice. It's a restriction; it's being imposed upon you. So thinking 'I can't' undermines your sense of power and personal agency."[5]

chapter wrap-up

There are several time-management strategies for preventing stress. Enhancing your time-management skills, preventing procrastination, delegating, and avoiding overcommitment can all help you reclaim hours in your day.

Do you have a to-do list that is mostly decorative? Do you find yourself browsing Facebook or shopping on Amazon at work? Do you cringe at the thought of delegating?

What if you had five more hours each week to devote to work? In this chapter, you've learned several helpful strategies to help prevent more acute stressors. The next step is building true resilience to stress. That is the key to living a stress-less life. It is also the focus of the next chapter.

build resilience: become the bendable bamboo

by building resilience, you can avoid being defined by stress. You can become the bamboo in the monsoon that bends rather than breaks.

This chapter is about the rest of your life. In the pages that follow, you'll learn how to build resilience against stress. You'll learn how some of the central concepts of your life, such as nature, time, and family, affect your longevity. And, more importantly, you'll become better-equipped to make fundamental changes to your life to promote longevity. Leadership is not a short-term gig. Without a long and healthy life, your impact won't live up to its potential.

longevity

Do you think about longevity? Do you yearn to see commercial space travel become a reality? It's human nature to want to live a long and healthy life, but stress conflicts with this desire. It thwarts longevity. After all, stress is a root cause of aging. There's a reason CEOs and presidents accumulate gray hair more quickly after they assume their new positions. The constant exposure to stress's harmful toxins shortens life expectancy, a phenomenon known as "inflammaging." There's a strong relationship between stress and life expectancy.

There are many components to longevity, and it's important to unpack and review them here. You'll recognize some of these from earlier chapters, as many of them also play a role in stress management and prevention. In this chapter, we'll explore how they relate to longevity.

exercise

We talked about the importance of exercise in controlling stress in Chapter 8, but exercise is directly linked to your longevity as well. The official causes of death tied to stress, such as heart disease and cancer, often mask the actual causes of death. The truth is that physical inactivity is near the top of the list. According to the World Health Organization (WHO), physical inactivity represents the fourth leading risk factor for death in the world.[1] Sedentary lifestyles are associated with a host of health conditions, including certain types of cancers, depression, cardiovascular disease, high blood pressure, high cholesterol levels, and coronary heart disease. Many of these negative health effects also affect people who aren't obese; being thin won't save you if you still don't exercise.

Exercise is a fabulous way to reduce age-related declines in cognitive and physical functions. Research has shown that regular physical activity can help slow the aging process and even predict successful aging. One study found that individuals who engaged in high levels of physical activity exhibited biological aging markers that appeared nine years younger than those who were sedentary.[2]

nutrition

Poor nutrition is another major cause of death. Approximately one in five deaths can be attributed to poor diet.[3] Poor-quality foods such as refined sugars cause inflammation and speed the aging process, and are, of course, part of the stress problem as well.

Fortunately, much like exercise, healthy diets can prevent and even reverse the aging process. For example, several studies have found that plant-rich vegan diets are linked to increased telomere length and increased telomerase activity. One study showed that diets rich in carotenoids (the pigments responsible for the bright colors of fruits and vegetables) are linked to longer telomeres,[4] which are key to the aging process. Studies consistently show that people with long telomeres live longer and healthier lives than individuals with short telomeres.

Remarkably, your perceptions of aging and the level of stress you associate with the aging process are closely linked to your longevity. As part of a study conducted by Becca Levy, a professor at the Yale School of Public Health, subjects were asked whether they agreed with statements such as, "Things keep getting worse as I get older," and, "As you get older, you are less useful." Those who agreed died an average of seven and a half years earlier than those who disagreed. Your outlook on aging has a tremendous impact on your ultimate longevity.[5]

pets

When it comes to stress, dogs (and other animals) are certainly humankind's best friend. Interacting with pets has been shown to increase cardiovascular health, increase confidence, and improve overall well-being. Animals and pets can serve as social support, providing a nonjudgmental ear. Tim (profiled in Chapter 3) has a cat that gives him tremendous joy and relief. Researchers have found that pets can have a calming effect on their owners and even lower blood pressure.[6] Adopting or taking care of pets can also have strong benefits for them, including saving their lives and quelling stress. You and the pet are bringing joy to each other, so who's taking care of who?

Depending on the animal, having a pet or an emotional support animal can have the added benefit of encouraging physical activity, reducing stress further. There's a reason that emotional support animals are recognized by the U.S. government as a key part of mental health treatment and are subject to certain housing and travel rights.

One study found that the simple act of stroking a living creature (no matter if it is furry, fuzzy, slimy, scaly, or hard-shelled) reduced anxiety levels. What's especially remarkable is that stroking a toy animal had no effect. Individuals who said they disliked animals even experienced the emotional effects as well! The act of petting animals promotes the release of serotonin, prolactin, and oxytocin, all hormones that boost mood, reduce depression, and quell stress.[7] These and similar studies have led many workplaces to embrace pet-friendly offices.

Do you have a furry (or scaled) friend? Do you notice that your mood and stress levels change when you're around it? If you don't have regular contact with an animal, would you consider adopting one or volunteering at a shelter? The added benefit is that you would be saving their life, too. Imagine that!

nature

How much time do you spend in nature? Does your work environment include "green" elements? Look around you right now. How many plants, trees, or other green things do you see?

In today's hyper-connected age, you don't have a lot of time to bask in the great outdoors. But surrounding yourself with nature can do wonders for reducing your stress levels and promoting longevity. Consider a study that involved participants going on a 90-minute walk, either through a natural or an urban environment. The researchers found that participants who walked through the natural environment reported lower levels of rumination, a common symptom of depression and anxiety.[8] They also showed decreased neural activity in an area of the brain associated with a greater risk of mental illness. A similar study found that participants who walked in a forest had lower blood pressure and cortisol levels afterward compared to participants who walked through a city environment.[9] This practice, called *Shinrin-yoku* or "forest-bathing," is heavily rooted in Japanese culture.

Fortunately, the benefits of nature can be realized in the workplace. One study found that workers situated near windows and indoor plants cited higher job satisfaction levels than employees situated farther away from these "green" elements.[10] Green elements have been shown to decrease frustration, anxiety, and turnover rates in the workplace.[11] Even indirect contact with nature is linked to lower stress levels and promotes clearer thinking. Recognizing this, some companies have installed screens throughout their workplaces depicting oceans, forests, and other nature settings.

time with children

Spending time with children can be delightful. Taking care of children marks a pivotal period of a person's life. That said, raising children can also take a heavy toll on your stress levels. From changing diapers to sleepless nights, it's not a pursuit for the undecided. But when you're armed with the right mindset and tool kit, it can promote longevity and prevent long-term stress. Research has found that parenting is associated with increased happiness and meaning in life. One study found that parents are happier when taking care of their children than while doing other daily activities.[12] Fathers, in particular, cited greater levels of happiness and meaning in life compared to childless individuals.

Stress starts at a young age. Parents play pivotal roles in how, and to what extent, stress affects their children. Research published in 1998 by Vincent Felitti and Robert Anda revealed that the effects of severe childhood stress can shorten your lifespan by 20 years.[13] Through their relationship with parents, children learn to trust and interact with others. When relationships are weak or unpredictable, children are more likely to view the world as unsafe, learn to resist authority figures, and lose trust in others. All this makes it more difficult for children to develop healthy relationships in the future, including with partners, teachers, and bosses.

Think back to your childhood. How stressful was your academic life? A key source of stress among children is school life and academics. One study found that nearly 40 percent of parents said their high school children were experiencing a lot of stress from school.[14] While some of this stress is caused by social issues and bullying, most is due to academics and the relationships (or lack thereof) between students and teachers.

travel

With or without children, people often associate travel with high stress. Missing a connecting flight or losing a piece of baggage can drive your stress to the sky. But traveling offers a lot of benefits in terms of reducing stress levels and increasing quality of life. Unfortunately, many people don't prioritize vacation time. Americans are half as likely as Europeans to travel abroad to visit more than one country.[15]

When was the last time you planned a leisure trip? Did you know the benefits of traveling can start before you even check in at the airport? One study found that the mere act of planning a trip increases your happiness levels.[16] The anticipation of the trip and the thrill associated with partaking in a novel experience can lift your mood.

The real benefits of travel, though, happen after you arrive at your destination. Traveling exposes you to new experiences. In exploring the world, your perspective expands, and by interacting with new cultures, you can see yourself more clearly through others' eyes. Traveling also gives you unique opportunities to learn about global history and heritage, which is critical to the future of the planet. Those who fail to learn history are doomed to repeat it.

Travel even expands your creative capacity. One study, led by Columbia Business School professor Adam Galinsky, found a clear relationship between the creative output of fashion designers and the time they spent abroad. He explained, "Foreign experiences increase both cognitive flexibility and depth and integrativeness of thought, the ability to make deep connections between disparate forms."[17]

Of course, travel has few benefits if you're cooped up in a hotel room working and stressing the whole time. To truly benefit from the increased stimulation that travel offers, you must immerse yourself in your destination. You must engage with the local culture to gain any type of creative boost.

What's stopping you from planning your next vacation?

time

Travel also changes your perception of time. Time is an ethereal concept. In 400 A.D., philosopher Saint Augustine wrote in his *Confessions*, "What is time? . . . Who can even form a conception of it to be put in words?" Humans have various mechanisms for perceiving time. Some are universal. People rise and retire with the rhythms of the sun, for example. Others are highly individualistic. "A long time ago" means something different to each person.

How would you answer the following question? "Next Wednesday's meeting has been moved forward two days. What day will the meeting be on?" Take a few seconds to think about it.

You probably answered either Friday or Monday. When researchers at Stanford University asked that question to travelers who had just gotten off a plane, they were more likely than non-travelers to say Friday.[18] Having just moved forward in actual physical space, the travelers were more likely to imagine forward motion in time as well. Even travelers about to board a plane were more likely to answer Friday. They were already imagining moving forward in space!

There's a strong relationship between your stress levels and your perception of time. In one study, participants found that time passed more slowly than usual during periods of relaxation than during periods of stress.[19] But they later remembered the time spent relaxing as being shorter. A fixation on the present was associated with lower levels of stress, while a fixation on the past was associated with higher levels of stress.

Having an accurate perception of time is critical to managing your stress levels. If you focus more strongly on past stressful events, you're likely to experience even higher levels of stress in the future. You may also experience higher levels of stress if you perceive future events to be happening sooner than they actually are since you will feel you have less time to plan and complete tasks.

Taking breaks is critical to restoring your perception of time and reducing your stress levels. One study found that workers who took short, frequent breaks reported higher levels of job satisfaction, reduced exhaustion, and greater willingness to go beyond their assigned tasks.[20] Research has even shown that your neurons become more resistant to diseases such as epilepsy and dementia when you allow for a period of rest after stressful events. You need time to recharge. Are you diligent about scheduling breaks into your days?

find your purpose

In his classic book *Man's Search for Meaning*, Viktor Frankl, an Austrian neurologist and psychiatrist, chronicled his experiences as a prisoner in the Auschwitz concentration camp during World War II. Frankl observed that those around him who did not lose their sense of purpose and meaning in life survived much longer than those who lost their way.

What is your purpose in life? Finding it is key to building resilience against stress. One study found that a greater sense of purpose is linked to lower levels of perceived stress.[21]

Your personality is shaped by your responses to certain psychosocial events, which involve a conflict between your individual psychological needs and what society needs. Developmental psychologist Erik Erikson's theory of psychosocial development states that your personality develops in a predetermined order following eight distinct stages. At each stage, you experience a psychosocial crisis, and your response, positive or negative, affects your personality. If you complete each stage successfully, you acquire basic key virtues and a stronger sense of self. This process ultimately helps you establish your life's purpose.

When people first enter the work force, many of them are in Erikson's sixth stage of psychosocial development: intimacy vs. isolation. This stage involves establishing intimate relationships with other people. These may be with partners or spouses or even with friends and co-workers. A failure to develop these intimate relationships results in isolation and loneliness and, in turn, impairs your ability to gain the virtue of love. (Your interpersonal finger should be twitching.)

Later in your career, you enter Erikson's seventh stage: generativity vs. stagnation. Generativity involves making an impact on the world that will extend beyond your own life. This is when many people identify their true purpose. They want to enact positive change in the world by raising children, volunteering for worthy causes, and becoming involved in community activities and organizations. If you fail to find a way to contribute to "the bigger picture," you may become stagnant and feel disconnected from society as a whole. But if you succeed, you feel a sense of pride and accomplishment and gain the virtue of care.

As you approach retirement, you embark on Erikson's final stage of psychosocial development: ego integrity vs. despair. This stage involves reflecting on your personal and professional accomplishments. If you're proud of what you've achieved, you feel a sense of integrity. You gain closure and obtain the virtue of wisdom. If you look back on your life with regret, you instead feel despair.

Your purpose in life is your compass. It will guide you. Finding your purpose involves determining what drives and energizes you. Unconstrained by financial or other concerns, if you could do only one thing for the rest of your life, what would it be? Consider the times you've experienced the greatest joy in your life. What were you doing?

The more you can align your personal and professional goals with your life's purpose, the more fulfilled you'll feel. Companies should recognize that each of their employees has a purpose in life and strive to create an environment that allows each employee to develop and realize his or her purpose.

Feeling a sense of purpose in the workplace is especially critical for attracting talent, especially among Millennials, who are likely to prioritize opportunities for social impact and de-emphasize monetary benefits. One study conducted by the Society for Human Resource Management found that 94 percent of Millennials want to use their skills to benefit a cause and 57 percent yearn for more companywide service days.[22] From volunteer days to corporate social responsibility (CSR) programs to diversity programs to eco-friendly initiatives, an organization's dedication to social impact matters.

diversity and belonging

Humans, in their pursuit of autonomy and privacy, have increasingly distanced themselves from their surroundings, and that's dangerous. Feeling that you belong is critical to coping with stress.

Find a safe space where you feel you belong—it may be your community, your neighbors, your volunteer group, or your racquetball club. There's a lot of comfort in knowing that you are not alone in your struggles, that you are included. Research indicates that people who don't know their neighbors are more likely to face serious health issues. Humans have a strong need to feel a connection to something bigger than ourselves. One enlightening study found that creating an increased sense of community belonging in tandem with developing a health-care policy that addresses the needs of those with specific health problems is a viable solution.[23]

You can also find a greater sense of belonging by feeling more connected to your familial roots. In the late 1990s, studies conducted by Emory University's Marshall Duke and colleagues revealed that children who possess a strong family narrative exhibit higher levels of emotional health.[24] The more children knew about their family history, the higher their levels of self-esteem and sense of control over their lives.

How strong is your sense of belonging? Do you feel a solid connection to your community? To your neighbors? Are you connected to your familial roots? How inclusive are you?

place work and stress in perspective

How clear is the divide between your personal and professional lives? So often, people's personal lives and work lives intermingle, and they stay glued to their work emails long after they've left the office. It certainly doesn't help that several U.S. companies, including Google, Apple, and Facebook, have established isolated, cult-like "campuses." When employees no longer need to go grocery shopping, pay their phone bills, do their laundry, or schedule haircuts, the cost is a loss of perspective—and an increase in stress.

It's critical to establish clear boundaries. Before leaving the physical office, tie up any loose ends and plan out the next day so you don't find yourself lying awake at night ruminating. Minimize work-related device use outside business hours. If you work from home, don't do it in a room you associate with family time. Shed your work attire as soon as you enter your house. Don't vent about your co-workers during dinnertime.

practice self-awareness

Self-awareness is another cornerstone of stress resilience. If you're unaware of your thoughts and feelings, they are more likely to control you. When you are aware of them, you can pause and make a decision before you act.

One of the most effective ways of increasing your self-awareness is through mindfulness training. Research suggests that mindful meditation practices can help ease psychological stress.[25] One especially powerful mindful meditation practice is the body scan. This consists of focusing on each body part one at a time and consciously letting go of any tension, including stomach knots or muscle tension, that you uncover. One study found that the time participants spent practicing the body scan was linked to lower levels of reactivity to stress.[26]

Give the body scan a try. Lie down in a quiet place, close your eyes, and give your attention and awareness to your head. Is your mouth dry? How does your chin feel? Move on to your neck. Do you feel tension? Does your jaw feel tight? Focus on relaxing it as much as possible. Are your biceps tight? Let them go limp. Move to your hands and fingers. Are your joints tight? Move on to your arms. Are your biceps tight? How do they feel? Move your back. Is it stiff? Proceed to your chest. Focus on your ribs as you inhale and exhale. Move on to your thighs. How do they feel? Proceed to your knees. Feel the muscles where they attach to your shin. Finish with your toes. Find your fourth toe on your right foot. Does it feel different than the rest?

help others

Performing acts of kindness for other people can help build resilience to stress. Research has shown that helping others dampens the effects of everyday stress[27] and can be achieved with even the simplest act: saying thank you. Gratitude has been proved to ward off a host of toxic emotions, including envy, resentment, regret, and depression, all of which trigger high levels of stress. Research has shown that gratitude is associated with 23 percent lower levels of cortisol and other stress hormones.[28]

Let your landlord know you appreciate her hard work. Thank the cashier at your neighborhood grocery store after a positive customer experience. Give your co-worker a pat on the back for speaking up in a meeting. The key to gratitude is specificity and authenticity. Clearly explain how a specific individual empowered you to succeed or led to your growth or betterment.

Helping others doesn't require a large-scale effort. Small acts of kindness can function as iron fortresses against high stress levels. A 2018 study found that performing random acts of kindness activates the release of dopamine, a feel-good neurotransmitter that prevents stress. The phenomenon is often referred to as a "helper's high."[29] Much like stress, kindness is contagious, and its benefits are realized by the givers as well as the recipients.

Think about small and large acts of kindness you could perform. In addition to quelling your own stress levels, acts of kindness will help your community. Volunteer at a homeless shelter. Offer to tutor kids at your local library. Help an elderly lady with directions. At work, offer to mentor a summer intern. Hold the elevator for a colleague. Volunteer to help establish your company's CSR program.

practice stoicism

There's a clear link between control and stress. When you experience self-doubt and a lack of control, your stress levels go into overdrive. As you gain more control over your work and your life, you become more resilient to stress.

In an effort to gain a stronger sense of control over their lives, many of today's most esteemed leaders, including Bill Clinton, J.K. Rowling, Tim Ferriss, and Jack Dorsey, have incorporated the ancient Greek philosophy of Stoicism into their daily lives. Stoicism advocates that you should only concern yourself with the events you can control. Stoics learn to distinguish between things that are under their control and things that are not. You can't control whether you'll be diagnosed with cancer. But you can control how you prepare for and respond to the treatment and recovery process.

One of the most common Stoic practices is negative visualization, which is closely tied to the "What's the worst that can happen?" exercise you read about in Chapter 3. Stoics habitually engage in negative visualization to reduce anxiety and stress. A 2007 study published in *Social and Personality Psychology Compass* found that individuals who practiced defensive pessimism experienced significantly higher levels of self-esteem.[30]

chapter wrap-up

Exercise, nutrition, animals, nature, taking care of children, travel, time, finding your purpose, diversity and belonging, placing work and stress in perspective, self-awareness, helping others, and Stoicism all affect your outlook on life and, ultimately, your longevity. They affect how you see the world and whether you wake up each day invigorated by a greater purpose. As the research shows, your perceptions of aging affect how well you age.

chapter 14

mission accomplished with the four "i"s

S tress is an unrelenting force, a primal "stone age" reaction that can propel you to new heights and horizons or bring you to an absolute standstill. Stress is also a universal concept. It knows no cultural, demographic, temporal, or geographic bounds. It affects each and every one of us.

Among leaders, stress is as commonplace as Monday morning meetings. You face a slew of different stressors throughout the day. While some stressors are similar to the ones everyone else experiences, several are unique to leaders. You've probably found yourself lacking the resources you need to do your job and dealing with unreasonable customer or co-worker demands.

Stress has an unprecedented influence on your personal and professional well-being. It results in a number of harmful physiological responses, which may be cognitive (such as impaired decision making), emotional (such as irritability), behavioral (such as social withdrawal), or physical (such as headaches). You now know that stress can prevent you from being productive, fostering healthy relationships, inspiring your team, and reaching your full potential.

We've reviewed each of your five stress fingers and showed you how to wave goodbye to stress. And we've learned about a host of different stress solutions to address your cognitive, emotional, interpersonal, physical, and spiritual fingers. By now you've recruited a stress buddy and started to experiment with different activities to discover which ones work best for you.

There is no magic bullet to eliminate all stress symptoms and prevent all stress. It's important to keep experimenting. Over time, you'll find you can wave goodbye to stress. Remember, to see progress you should commit to at least two fingers at any given time.

Over the years of working with leaders and companies, I've found that a leader's ability to conquer stress depends on four steps. These four steps are what I want to leave you with—they help bring together all the techniques and experiments we have covered so far to give you a springboard for action. I call them the Four "I"s: Ignite, Initiate, Implement, and Inspire.

1. ignite

It's easy to think of stress as a natural part of life, an inevitable and uncontrollable force. But you must strive for positive change. You must be willing to be vulnerable and make a conscious effort to look deeply within and outside yourself. In your quest to become an effective leader, aspire to address stress at the individual and organizational level, recognizing that the former must be tackled before the latter. You must ignite your exploration of the role stress plays in your leadership life.

2. initiate

Once you're willing to address stress, the next question is, "How do I start the effort?" Dealing with stress requires a multipronged approach. At the personal level, you must identify your internal stressors, such as pessimism or perfectionism, and your external stressors, such as disgruntled customers or insufficient resources. At the organizational level, a similar degree of awareness must exist. You can diagnose stress using assessments, surveys, interviews, and other means to truly understand the nature of the problem.

To initiate a successful stress-management effort, acknowledgment is critical. Techniques such as the "What's the worst that can happen?" exercise we discussed in Chapter 3 can motivate leaders to take action by recognizing that the cost of inaction is high.

Effective leaders drive stress management by taking advantage of the brain's neuroplasticity. As the research indicates, the damage induced by stress can be repaired, and the brain can be rewired. To truly wave goodbye to stress, leaders must attack from all five angles: cognitively, emotionally, interpersonally, physically, and spiritually. Logic games or memory challenges can improve your ability to concentrate and remember key information and enhance your cognitive functioning. Enhanced listening, self-awareness, and recognizing your perspective enable you to gain high levels of emotional intelligence and boost your emotional capacity. Increased social skills strengthen your interpersonal relationships and improve your team's morale. A focus on exercise, better sleep patterns, and healthy diets boosts your energy levels and improves your physical functioning. Finally, prayer, meditation, and other spiritual rituals are key to finding your purpose in life and waking up inspired each morning.

All this allows leaders to begin their stress resistance effort and figure out how they will deal with stress on a daily basis. This is often the most challenging part of the process, as it is unfamiliar territory and requires a lot of growing pains. Rest assured that with a dedicated effort, you can succeed. All you have to do is start.

3. implement

As leaders continue in their quest, they must put a plan in place to deal with daily stress. This is the implementation phase. A key component of implementation involves prevention. While leaders must learn to cope with stress, they must also put strategies in place to prevent stress from rearing its ugly head.

At the organizational level, successful implementation involves many components and is best facilitated by an executive coach.

4. inspire

A leader's ultimate objective is to inspire a life of stress-less leadership. Stress has a profound influence on your longevity. To gain resilience against stress, you must consider the various aspects of your life, including pets, travel, time, belonging, and nature, that affect your longevity. Stress influences how you see the world and whether you wake up each day invigorated by a greater purpose.

Inspiring a life of stress-less leadership includes creating organizational change. Your work environment has a profound impact on your longevity. From job security to health insurance to wellness programs, workplace policies affect your well-being. You can drive efforts to develop an EAP or implement wellness programs such as yoga classes to inspire a stress-less environment. Great companies consider time-off policies, pay inequality, benefits, and other aspects of their business when creating policies to combat stress.

final words

This book sprang from a deep quest in myself and in my clients for solutions that address stress and leadership at both the individual and organizational levels. I hope the lessons and activities in this book have inspired, educated, and entertained you. If you take the lessons from this book to heart, you will overcome your individual stressors and advance your abilities as a leader. Be brave, be bold, be kind.

I carry all those who suffer from stress in my heart, and I hope you will carry this book, a part of me, in your heart, too. I hope you always remember that five-fingered wave to wave away your stress. Maybe you will remember our journey as you catch a glimpse of your hand in your daily life. I hope the stress solutions in this book fill the void in the current resource offerings on the topic, and I hope you will share your experiments and their results with others.

You are now well on your way to conquering stress for the rest of your life. I applaud your courage, your persistence, and your drive to improve yourself and your situation. Please take good care of yourself and others as you go about your experiments.

endnotes

introduction

[1] Marlin Company and The American Institute of Stress (2011). Attitudes in the American workplace VII [PDF].

chapter 1

[1] https://en.wikipedia.org/wiki/Yerkes%E2%80%93Dodson_law

2 Marlin Company and The American Institute of Stress (2011). Attitudes in the American workplace VII [PDF].

3 American Migraine Foundation (n.d.). Stress and migraine [PDF].

4 American Heart Association and American Stroke Association (2018). Heart disease and stroke statistics at-a-glance 2018 [PDF].

5 Shockey, T.M. and Wheaton, A.G. (2017). Short sleep duration by occupation group — 29 States, 2013–2014. MMWR Morb Mortal Wkly, 66, 207–213.

6 Buettner, Dan (2012). Are you heart hungry? *Psychology Today.*

7 Campbell, Michael, et al. (2015). The stress of leadership [PDF].

8 Biggs, David (n.d.). Poor employee relations and its effect on customer demand [PDF].

9 Cornerstone on Demand (n.d.). Toxic employees in the workplace: hidden costs and how to spot them [PDF].

10 Job stress is more strongly associated with health complaints than financial or family problems.

11 www.cdc.gov/niosh

12 The American Institute of Stress (n.d.). America's #1 health problem.

chapter 2

1 American Psychological Association Center for Organizational Excellence (n.d.). Work stress.

2 Remes, O., Brayne, C.E., van, d. L.R., and Lafortune, L. (2016). A systematic review of reviews on the prevalence of anxiety disorders in adult populations. Brain and Behavior.

3 American Psychology Association (n.d.). Gender and stress.

4 Petrone, Paul (2018). Stress at work: see who's feeling it the most and how to overcome it.

chapter 3

[1] Barnfield, Heather, ed. (2014). *FYI: For Your Improvement - Competencies Development Guide*, 6th Edition. Los Angeles: Korn Ferry.

[2] White, Randall (2010). Ambiguity leadership: it's okay to be uncertain.

[3] Seagal, Jeanne, et al. (2018). Stress symptoms, signs, and causes: improving your ability to handle stress.

[4] Kinnunen, U., Feldt, M., Siltaloppi, M., Sonnentag S. (2011). Job demands-resources model in the context of recovery: Testing recovery experiences as mediators. *European Journal of Work and Organizational Psychology*, 20. 805–32.

[5] TUISKU, Katinka, et al. (2016). Cultural leisure activities, recovery and work engagement among hospital employees. Industrial Health 54.3, 254–262.

[6] Mayo Clinic Staff (2018). Social support: tap this tool to beat stress.

[7] American Psychological Association (2014). Stress Report [PDF].

chapter 5

[1] Yarow, Jay (2015). AOL's CEO makes his executives spend 10% of their time just thinking every day. *Business Insider*.

[2] Feloni, Richard (2017). The CEO of Airbnb starts each morning with a simple but effective twist on the standard to-do list. *Business Insider*.

[3] Didner, Pam (2015). A look inside Intel's annual planning process.

chapter 6

[1] Sehryan, F. (2007). The impact of emotional intelligence skills training on how to deal with psychological stress. *Research Psychology Journal of Tabriz University 2(8)*:70–84.

2 Career Builder (2011). Seventy-one percent of employers say they value emotional intelligence over IQ.

3 Davies, Rob (2016). How Zolando sets goals.

chapter 7

1 Globoforce (2014). Workforce mood tracker fall 2014 report: the effect of work relationships on organizational culture and commitment [PDF].

2 Folkman, Zenger (2017). Three signs you are a counterfeit bold leader and how to improve.

chapter 8

1 Coulson, J.C., McKenna, J., and Field, M. (2008). Exercising at work and self-reported work performance. *International Journal of Workplace Health Management 1(3):* 176-197.

2 Beezhold, B., et al. (2015). Vegans report less stress and anxiety than omnivores. *Nutritional Neuroscience, 18(7):* 289-96.

3 Kuhn, Marion et al. (2016). Sleep recalibrates homeostatic and associative synaptic plasticity in the human cortex. *Nature Communications* (2016).

chapter 9

1 Borchard, Therese (2010). Spirituality and prayer stress relief. *Huffington Post.*

2 Seppala, Emma M. (2016). The surprising health benefits of spirituality. *Psychology Today.*

3 Pew Research Center (2016). Many Americans overeat, few meditate to cope with stress.

[4] Kirk, U., Downar, J., and Montague, P. (2011). Interoception drives increased raotional decision-making in meditators playing the ultimatum game. *Frontiers Neuroscience.*

chapter 10

[1] Harvard T.H. Chan School of Public Health. (2016). More than four in 10 working adults think their work impacts their health: Most say their workplace is supportive of actions to improve their health. *ScienceDaily.*

[2] Pazzanese, Christina (2016). The high price of workplace stress. *The Harvard Gazette.*

[3] CareerCast reveals the top stressful jobs to have in 2018 (2018).

[4] Health Advocate, Inc. (n.d.). Stress in the workplace [PDF].

[5] Health Advocate, Inc. (n.d.). Stress in the workplace [PDF].

[6] The American Institute of Stress (n.d.). Workplace stress.

[7] International Employee Assistance Professionals Association (n.d.). Frequently asked questions.

[8] Chestnut Global Partners (2016). Trend report 2016 [PDF].

[9] Clavelle, P.R., Dickerson, S.J., Murphy, M.W. (2012). Counseling outcomes at a U.S. Department of Defense employee assistance program. *Journal of Workplace Behavioral Health 27(3):*127-138.

[10] Selvik, Stephenson, Plaza, and Sugden, B. (2004). EAP impact on work, relationship, and health outcomes. *Journal of Employee Assistance*, 34(2): 18-22.

[11] Attridge, M., Amaral, T., Bjornson, T., et al. (2009). EAP effectiveness and ROI. *EASNA Research Notes 1(3):*1-5.

[12] Chestnut Global Partners (2016). Trend report 2016.

13 Can workplace wellness signal superior stock performance? (2016).

14 http://www.ifebp.org/pdf/ushealthyworkforce.pptx

15 Taylor, Tess (2016). Twenty-two percent of companies now offering mindfulness training.

16 Fernandez, Rich (2016). Help your team manage stress, anxiety, and burnout. *Harvard Business Review.*

17 O'Malley, Sharon (2017). Issue: paid leave; more companies offering unlimited time off. *SAGE Business Researcher.*

18 Achor, Shawn and Gielan, Michelle (2016). The data-driven case for vacation. *Harvard Business Review.*

19 O'Malley, Sharon (2017). Issue: paid leave; more companies offering unlimited time off. *SAGE Business Researcher.*

20 U.S. Travel Association (2018). State of American vacation 2018.

21 American Society of Interior Designers (2005). *Sound solutions: Increasing office productivity through integrated acoustic planning and noise reduction strategies.* Washington, DC: American Society of Interior Designers.

22 American Society of Interior Designers (2005). *Sound solutions: Increasing office productivity through integrated acoustic planning and noise reduction strategies.* Washington, DC: American Society of Interior Designers.

23 Health Advocate, Inc. (n.d.). Stress in the workplace [PDF].

chapter 11

1 Witvliet, Charlotte and Ludwig, Thomas and L. Vander Laan, Kelly (2001). Granting forgiveness or harboring grudges: implications for emotion, physiology, and health. *Psychological Science, 12*: 117-23.

[2] Fillon, Mike (2000). Holding a grudge can be bad for your health. *Web MD.*

[3] Fillon, Mike (2000). Holding a grudge can be bad for your health. *Web MD.*

[4] Toussaint, Loren L., Owen, Amy D., and Cheadle, Alyssa (2012). Forgive to live: forgiveness, health, and longevity. *Journal of Behavioral Medicine 35.4:* 375–386.

[5] Toussaint, L., Shields, G.S., Dorn, G., Slavich, G.M. (2016). Effects of lifetime stress exposure on mental and physical health in young adulthood: How stress degrades and forgiveness protects health. *Journal of Health Psychology, 21(6):*1004-1014.

[6] Fetzer Institute (n.d.). Fetzer survey on love and forgiveness in American Society.

[7] Mayo Clinic Staff (2017). Forgiveness: letting go of grudges and bitterness.

[8] Hodgson, L. K. and Wertheim, E. H. (2007). Does good emotion management aid forgiving? Multiple dimensions of empathy, emotion management and forgiveness of self and others. *Journal of Social and Personal Relationships*, 24(6), 931–949.

[9] Baylor University (2014). Letting it go: Take responsibility, make amends, forgive yourself. *ScienceDaily.*

[10] Gyllensten, K. and Palmer, S. (2006). Experiences of coaching and stress in the workplace: an interpretive phenomenological analysis. *International Coaching Psychology Review 1:* 86–98.

[11] Gyllensten, K. and Palmer, S. (2006). Experiences of coaching and stress in the workplace: an interpretive phenomenological analysis. *International Coaching Psychology Review 1:* 86–98.

chapter 12

[1] Grant, Heidi (2013). How are you motivated? A new free online diagnostic.

2 Avanzi, Lorenzo and Zaniboni, Sara and Fraccaroli, Franco and Balducci, Cristian (2014). The relation between overcommitment and burnout: Does it depend on employee job satisfaction?. *Anxiety, Stress, and Coping 27*: 455-465.

3 Babcock, Linda, Recalde, Maria P., Vesterlund, Lise, and Weingart, Laurie (2017). Gender differences in accepting and receiving requests for tasks with low promotability." *American Economic Review, 107 (3):* 714-47.

4 Patrick, V. and Hagtvedt, H. (2011). "I don't" versus "I can't": When empowered refusal motivates goal-directed behavior. *Journal of Consumer Research.*

5 Grant, Heidi (2013). How are you motivated? A new free online diagnostic.

chapter 13

1 World Health Organization (n.d.). Physical activity.

2 Tucker, L. (2017). Physical activity and telomere length in U.S. men and women : An NHANES investigation. *Preventive Medicine 100:* 145-151.

3 GBD 2017: A fragile world (2018). *The Lancet.*

4 Min, K.B. and Min, J.Y. (2017). *European Journal of Nutrition 56:* 1045.

5 Lachs, Mark (2011). Want to live to 100? Try to bounce back from stress.

6 Health Advocate, Inc. (n.d.). Stress in the workplace [PDF].

7 UCLA Health (n.d.). Animal-assisted therapy research findings.

8 Bratman, G. N., Hamilton, J. P., Hahn, K. S., Daily, G. C., and Gross, J. J. (2015). Nature experience reduces rumination and subgenual prefrontal cortex activation. *Proceedings of*

the National Academy of Sciences of the United States of America, 112(28), 8567-72.

9 Park, B.J., et al. (2010). The physiological effects of Shinrin-yoku (taking in the forest atmosphere or forest bathing): evidence from field experiments in 24 forests across Japan. *Environmental Health Preventative Medicine* 15 (1): 18026.

10 Health Advocate, Inc. (n.d.). Stress in the workplace [PDF].

11 Health Advocate, Inc. (n.d.). Stress in the workplace [PDF].

12 Brogaard, B. (2015). Does being a parent really make you happier? *Psychology Today.*

13 Cocozza, P. (2017). How childhood stress can knock 20 years off your life. *The Guardian.*

14 Harvard School of Public Health, Robert Wood Foundation, and NPR (2014). Education and health in schools: A survery of parents [PDF].

15 Otis, G. (2015). Americans half as likely as Europeans to travel to more than one country, and and 29% have never been abroad. *Daily News.*

16 Kumar, A., Killingsworth, M. A., and Gilovich, T. (2014). Waiting for merlot: anticipatory consumption of experiential and material purchases. *Psychological Science*, 25 (10), 1924–1931.

17 Crane, B. (2015). For a more creative brain, travel. *The Atlantic.*

18 Cooperrider, K. and Nunez, R. (2016). How we make sense of time. *Scientific American.*

19 Chavez, Bonnie R. (2019). Effects of stress and relaxation on time perception. 215.

20 Hunter, E.M. and Wu, C. (2016). Give me a better break: Choosing workday break activities to maximize resource recovery. *Journal of Applied Psychology.*

[21] Guzman, Anne. (2017). The role of perceived stress in the relationship between purpose in life and mental health.

[22] Gurchiek, K. (2014). Millennial's desire to do good defines workplace culture.

[23] Baiden, P., den Dunnen, W., Arku, G., et al. (2014) The role of sense of community belonging on unmet health care needs Ontario, Canada: findings from the 2012 Canadian community health survey. *Journal of Public Health* 22: 467–468.

[24] Bohanek, J., et al. (2006). Family narrative interaction and children's sense of self. *Family Process* 45 (1): 39-54.

[25] Goyal, M., Singh, S., Sibinga, E.M.S., et al. (2014). Meditation programs for psychological stress and well-being: a systematic review and meta-analysis. *JAMA Internal Medicine* 174(3): 357–368.

[26] Carmody, James and Baer, Ruth (2008). Relationships between mindfulness practice and levels of mindfulness, medical and psychological symptoms and well-being in a mindfulness-based stress reduction program. *Journal of Behavioral Medicine* 31: 23-33.

[27] Raposa, E. B., Laws, H. B., and Ansell, E. B. (2016). Prosocial behavior mitigates the negative effects of stress in everyday life. *Clinical Psychological Science,* 4(4): 691–698.

[28] UC Davis Health (2015). Gratitude is good medicine.

[29] http://psycnet.apa.org/record/2016-19956-001

[30] Norem, J. (2008). Defensive pessimism, anxiety, and the complexity of self-regulation. *Social and Personality Psychology Compass* 2 (1): 121–134.

about the author

dr. Nadine Greiner, Ph.D. is an executive coach, consultant, and speaker in San Francisco, California. Her Stress-Less workshops have taken the world by storm. Dr. Nadine's mission is to make the executive experience exceptionally enjoyable and effective. She believes that the world needs great leaders, so she has dedicated her career to helping them.

As a former corporate CEO, Dr. Nadine understands the pressures and demands executives face. She offers her clients the high expertise that only comes with decades of consulting success and a dual Ph.D. in Organization Development and Clinical Psychology.

Dr. Nadine is an in-demand speaker and teaches in doctoral programs. She is also the author of *The Art of Executive Coaching: Secrets to Unlock Leadership Potential*, in which she helps improve the coaching skills of other executive coaches.

On a personal note, Dr. Nadine is married to a scientist. She is also dedicated to animal welfare, and 100 percent of her proceeds of this book go to animals. Dr. Nadine stays fit by running after them all and by joining the dance party with her friends at Zumba.

Index